God, Gödel, and Grace

A Philosophy of Faith

God, Gödel, and Grace

A Philosophy of Faith

Clifford Goldstein

REVIEW AND HERALD® PUBLISHING ASSOCIATION
HAGERSTOWN, MD 21740

The author assumes full responsibility for the accuracy of all facts and quotations as cited in this book.

Texts credited to NIV are from the *Holy Bible, New International Version.* Copyright © 1973, 1978, 1984, International Bible Society. Used by permission of Zondervan Bible Publishers.

Bible texts credited to RSV are from the Revised Standard Version of the Bible, copyright © 1946, 1952, 1971, by the Division of Christian Education of the National Council of the Churches of Christ in the U.S.A. Used by permission.

This book was
Edited by Richard W. Coffen
Copyedited by James Cavil
Cover designed and illustrated by GenesisDesign
Interior designed by Tina M. Ivany
Typeset: Bembo 11/14

PRINTED IN U.S.A.

07   06   05   04   03   5   4   3   2   1

R&H Cataloging Service
Goldstein, Clifford, 1955-
    God, Gödel, and grace: a philosophy of faith.

    1. Religion—Philosophy.   I. Title.

                    210

ISBN 0-8280-1729-8

To all
whose desire for truth
transcends the joy of seeking it.

[Contents]

[Chapter 1]

Trinkets of Death

After a French office worker who had murdered an Arab on a hot, breathless Algerian beach was sentenced to have his "head cut off in a public square in the name of the French people,"[1] a chaplain entered the doomed man's cell. Not wanting to talk, Meursault said right away that he didn't believe in God. The chaplain, a Catholic priest, begged him to reconsider, asking if he really expected that when he died—that was it?

"Yes," Meursault answered.

When the priest asked him to look into the stones of the cell for the "divine face," Meursault replied that the only face he sought was "the flame of desire" from his former lover; but not even that, he said, much less the divine, emerged from "the sweating stones." When the priest offered to pray for him, Meursault shook him by the collar and screamed that all the chaplain's certainties weren't worth one hair on a woman's head, and that all people, even the priest, were going to die anyway, so what difference did it make? *Nothing*, Meursault screamed, not who was innocent or guilty, not whom one married, not even who one's friends were, *nothing mattered!* After the guards pulled Meursault off the chaplain and he left, the prisoner calmed down, dozing before being awakened by the night.

"Sounds of the countryside were drifting in. Smells of night, earth, and salt air were cooling my temples. The wondrous peace of that sleeping summer flowed through me like a tide. Then, in the dark hour before dawn, sirens blasted. They were announcing departures for a world that now and forever meant nothing to me. . . . For the first time, in that night alive with signs and stars, I opened myself to the gentle indifference of the world."[2]

That scene, exhumed from the last gasps of *The Stranger*, expressed Albert Camus' estrangement from what he called "this absurd, godless world,"[3] which taunts us with intimations of meaning and purpose, yet—spinning at more than 1,000 miles per hour—moves too fast for us to nuzzle any. Every attempt to rifle purpose from the bowels of the earth cedes, it seems, only dirt, worms, and the trinkets of death.

Logic is easy; logic taken to its conclusion isn't. That's what Camus did with Meursault. He wrenched his logic, however bitter, to the end, which is precisely why Meursault didn't express ordinary human pain. People rarely distend logic that far. (It is too bitter.)

Before the murder, when offered a better job, Meursault said it didn't matter what he did, because "one life was as good as another." When his girlfriend asked him to marry her, he said that "it didn't make any difference to me and that we could if she wanted to."[4] And he didn't really care that he would soon die, because the world "forever meant nothing" to him.

These were the paper-and-ink answers of a paper-and-ink concoction—a metaphor for cold logic, not for flesh and blood, because flesh and blood *knows* that one life isn't as good as another, *knows* that it matters whom we marry, *knows* that this world means something even if we're unsure what or why but only that it does, it must, it has to.

The finger has a purpose, the eye has a purpose, the ear has a purpose, the air has a purpose, the sun has a purpose—and yet these and untold other "purposes," so finely and majestically woven, culminate into purposelessness? More finely tuned than Bach's *Fantasia,* more complex than Boolean algebra, and deeper dimensionally than Michelangelo's *Creazione di Adamo*—this creation, nevertheless, culminates into nothing? "The more the universe seems comprehensible," wrote physicist Steven Weinberg, "the more it seems pointless."[5] But how can so many individual and finite things—replete with points, and opulent with purpose themselves—so beautifully, precisely, and artfully climax into blunt nothingness? It's like a string of positive integers equaling zero.

Humanity's worst fear is discovering not that we've got the meaning wrong but that there is none. We're rubbed by what South African Laurens van der Post called "the burden of meaninglessness,"[6] this subtle nudge that we are stranded, third rock from the sun, in a cold, dead universe that will one day fold back on itself and suck into oblivion all endeavors, loves, passions, and dreams that floated along its surface like reflections on the eyes of a corpse.

The cosmos is mostly empty space. ("The eternal silence of these infinite spaces," wrote Pascal, "fills me with dread.")[7] We—our minds, our bodies—are composed of particles so small in comparison to the gaps between them that even our deepest thoughts are like specks of dust in pillaged cathedrals. Einstein proved with a formula so simple it can be read off a T-shirt at 20 paces that even the little material blemishing the universe is convertible into energy—mass less photons, nothing else. In the quantum realm, the realm upon which all that's physical rests, reality is so nebulous, so statistical and spectral, that physicists question if anything is real.

No wonder people fear their meaninglessness; they have good reason to. "The elementary laws," wrote Walt Whitman, "never apologize."[8] And certainly never to us.

Nevertheless something gnaws at this aura of meaninglessness, something sticks to our consciences like candy to our teeth, alluding (but never *more* than alluding) to a formula beneath the ferment. If nothing else, "existence" alone contains within itself the concept of "meaning"; to exist is to mean, even if the meaning is unknown or even unknowable. To mean *nothing* is, still, to mean.

Yet what's worse? To sense with the heart purpose yet with the mind never to know it; or, like Meursault, to deny the purpose altogether, even when it whispers to us from the throats of deep roses that disappear in dark winds, when it flashes before us in dreams washed away by fresh morning light, when it mocks us with the geometrical precision of the fractal, or when it cries to us with throats thickening from selfless acts of love and mercy? Only a soul made of paper and ink, like Meursault, could ignore all these hints and reconcile itself up to the "gentle indifference of the world." Souls made of flesh and blood can't. The world, they know, is neither gentle nor indifferent but has pitted them in a losing struggle against gravity (the weakest of the four forces of nature), which constantly and mercilessly yanks them downward, earthward (the closer to the earth the greater the pull, so even in the grave the drag's the hardest).

Downward, earthward, however, is where, said Nietzsche, we belong, because there's nothing else, anywhere else, for us, especially beyond the stars. "I beseech you, my brothers," his Zarathustra proclaimed, *"remain faithful to the earth,* and do not believe those who speak to you of other-worldly hopes!"[9] Though the greatest sin had once been the sin against God, God died, and thus saith Zarathustra—"to sin against the earth is now the most dreadful thing, and to esteem the entrails of the unknowable higher than the meaning of the earth."[10]

For Nietzsche, the situation was simple: "The Christian God has ceased to be believable."[11] Though an unabashed atheist who hated Christianity (he once dubbed himself the Anti-Christ), Nietzsche nevertheless foresaw the profound, and fearful, consequences of this loss of belief. He understood that the West cannot give up the Christian God and continue as if nothing epochal had happened. That churches would become museums, or crosses artifacts, or priests shoe salesmen—this was inconsequential, mere detritus, nothing more.

Instead, Nietzsche saw that all which leaned up this God and His institutions, all which grew up on this God and His moral commandments, all which nourished itself upon this God and His promises, and all which understood itself in relationship to this God and His sovereignty—this would all crumble, leaving hordes of refugees burrowed amid the decomposing corpse of deity. (Gods too, claimed Nietzsche, decompose.)[12] And what cold monster, what infernal beast, would arise from the remains?

It wasn't just that God was dead. For Nietzsche, all metaphysics was dead, all belief in any overarching metanarrative, any transcendent bond that could tie it all together and deliver it in a neat, mathematically precise package, any conception of divine ordering. It was all gone, killed by the ones who for centuries had greedily sucked life, hope, and meaning from its distended belly. Truth, said Nietzsche, was nothing but canonized illusions, metaphors that had petrified, and traditions that had become cultural addictions and ethnic habits. The only truth was that there was no Truth, the only certainly was that there was no certainty. No eternal harmonies serenaded the spheres—only random, discordant tones and rhythms ricocheting through interstellar chaos like a piano heaved down the stairs.

"How were we able to drink up the sea?" asked Nietzsche (through the words of a madman who, with a lantern in his hand, ran into the marketplace). "Who gave us the sponge to wipe away the entire horizon? What did we do when we unchained this earth from its sun? Whither is it moving now? Whither are we moving now? Away from all suns? Are we not plunging continually? Backward, sideward, forward, in all directions? Is there any up or down left? Are we not straying as through an infinite nothing? Do we not feel the breath of empty space? Has it not become colder?"[13]

For centuries our ancestors would climb the squat stone steps of ziggurats in order to get closer to the stars so they could better discern the secrets hidden behind those cold, distant fires. Today refractors and reflectors have shown that those same insensate flames are so far away from us that there's little chance of finding truth for ourselves within their epicyclical loops. That's why Zarathustra loved those "who do not first seek behind the stars."[14] The stars are inaccessible, and even if we could reach that far, nothing's there for us anymore. Meaning, purpose, truth, if to be found, have to be dredged out of the earth or trumped up from among ourselves, because God is dead—"and we," Nietzsche charged, "have killed him."[15]

Aristotle wrote that we can't understand anything without knowing its causes; that must include humanity, too. Until about a century and a half ago, we mostly understood ourselves as coming, in one way or another, from God; now we understand ourselves as slowly clawing our way out of our skin and torturously breaking free from the bones of untutored primates. It's a seismic shift in human self-understanding to look in the mirror and—rather than seeing an image of the Lord God Yahweh, Creator of the heavens and the earth—having the latest variant mutation of natural selection stare back in our faces instead. This revised reflection, and all that it does to the human ego and sense of self-worth, contains (Nietzsche saw) predicates of colossal consequences.

Nor did he alone see the results of this new genesis. Jean-Paul Sartre, the twentieth century's most influential atheist, said: "It is very distressing that God does not exist, because all possibility of finding values in a heaven of ideas disappears along with Him; there can no longer be an *a priori* Good, since there is no infinite and perfect consciousness to think it."[16]

Philosopher Bertrand Russell wrote that "many traditional ethical concepts are difficult to interpret, and many traditional ethical beliefs are hard to justify, except on the assumption that there is a God or a World Spirit or at least an immanent cosmic Purpose."[17]

Atheist apologist J. L. Mackie argued that "moral properties constitute so odd a cluster of qualities and relations that they are most unlikely to have arisen in the ordinary course of events without an all-powerful god to create them."[18] (Mackie solved his problem by denying the properties.)

In a godless universe, asked Fyodor Dostoyevsky, where would morality come from? (Or, as he had Mitya Karamazov express it: "Well, but you, without a God, are more likely to raise the price of meat, if it suits you, and make a rouble on every copeck.")[19]

The Truth, or the Good (whatever those terms now mean), no longer permeates the world as do the Pythagorean theorem, the laws of thermodynamics, or Planck's constant; morals are not like special or general relativity, fundamental facts of reality waiting thousands of years for Albert Einstein to extract them from the air. Instead, morality is as subjective and personal as fingerprints; perhaps it's mere cultural and personal biases more dependent upon childhood relationships than transcendent norms.

There is no "ought," only "is," and from this "is" no "ought" can be absolutely derived. With God dead, moral *knowledge* can't exist, only moral *belief.* Morality is preference, such as choosing Beethoven's Third Symphony over David Bowie's *Rise and Fall of Ziggy Stardust and the Spiders From Mars,* or Big Macs over clams casino. Values are judged by their utility—"good" gets the trains to run on time; "bad" causes them to be late. Or even less fundamental: "good" is what you like; "bad" is what you don't.

Human senses (not divine commandments), human appetites (not sacred texts), and human desires (not religious injunctions), these are the stuff that morality—good, evil, right, and wrong—is made of, because there is nothing else. Truth is horizontal, not vertical; it's physical, not spiritual; it comes from mitosis, testosterone, and protein metabolism, not from the Father, Son, and Holy Ghost. Values have to be contrived from among ourselves, concocted out of a boiling brew of human passion, flesh, and dreams, and not revealed by some brooding omnipresence in the sky. As players in a game, we make up the rules as we go along; we must, because the primates didn't leave behind detailed instructions.

Of course, Bertrand Russell, Friedrich Nietzsche, Jean-Paul Sartre, and J. L. Mackie knew that it was wrong to torture little children. Many atheists and secularists have been, still are, and will be "good" people, at times even "better" than their religious counterparts. (After all, when was the last time a skeptic strapped himself full of explosives and took out a city bus?) That atheists and secularists can devise internally coherent moral systems is not the issue; the issue, instead, is what they *can't* do: derive an internally coherent moral system based upon any transcendent or immutable absolute—because, they assert (often absolutely), none exists.

A system is only as stable as its foundation. Why build a house on pink elephants when nothing more than a purple turtle could knock it down? We work only with what's available, and for the secularist, the atheist, what's available is only conditional, relative, human, nothing more because there is nothing else.

If values are derived from humanity, from human needs, from human nature, from human desires alone, because these needs, natures, and desires are malleable, fluctuating, and transient—all morals systems based on them must be as well. Maybe that's good; maybe values should change along with desires and needs; maybe morals should fluctuate with the weather or the moon. Maybe there should be no moral axioms, only moral hypotheses; no moral imperatives, only moral hunches; no moral commands, only moral urges. Maybe truth is more poetic than geometric, more hormonal than metaphysical, more like wind than rocks. If so, then one must admit that, given specific circumstances, torturing little children might be the moral thing to do. Who can say with terminal certainty that it's wrong when, working only with the conditional and the relative, you can never say anything but the conditional and the relative?

Dostoyevsky grappled with these questions so fervently that the pages of *Crime and Punishment* stick together with the sweat of his moral turmoil. Sofya Semyonovna Marmeladov becomes a prostitute in order to feed her starving little brother and sister. Rodion Romanovitch Raskolnikov kills a nasty, spiteful old usurer and steals her money in order to help his mother and sister, to advance his studies, and to become someone great who will devote himself to "the service of humanity and the good of all."[20]

Were these acts, given the intense circumstances that framed them, wrong? Was Rodion Romanovitch right when he said that "a single misdeed is permissible if the principal aim is right, a solitary wrongdoing and hundreds of good deeds"?[21] If there be no God who has imposed an immutable moral order on the universe, on what grounds can one, categorically, condemn murder and prostitution? What authority can, justly, impose these moral restraints upon autonomous souls?

The state? Perhaps. Yet what the state imposes the state can take away. If moral values are created by political fiat only, then they are technically no different than tax codes and speed limits. If the state (whether via a politburo or plebiscite) decides that murdering usurious old women in order to help mothers and sisters, or prostituting oneself in order to feed hungry children, is legal, or even moral—who's to say that they're wrong, and with what justification can one say it?

After her brother Polyneices was killed in a revolt, Antigone refused Theban King Creon's order that he not be buried. When brought before Creon, who demanded to know why she disobeyed his order, Antigone replied:

> Sorry, who made this edict? Was it God?
> Isn't a man's right to a burial decreed
> By divine justice? I don't consider your
> Pronouncements so important that they can
> Just . . . overrule the unwritten laws of heaven.
> You are a man, remember.
> These divine laws are not just temporary measures.
> They stand forever.[22]

Did Antigone's (or anyone's) brother deserve a decent burial, or should his (or anyone's) corpse have been left to the ravenous appetite of dogs and birds? If he deserved a burial, why? What grounds should supersede a *king's* decree? Do some moral codes, some "unwritten laws of heaven," decree that he (or anyone) must be buried? Or were Antigone's "divine laws" nothing but codified traditions and cultural trends that became "truth" through nothing but incessant, common use, such as red lights for stop and green for go?

If morality does not transcend the human, even the human manifested as the state, then Hitler's murder of the Jews in lands under Nazi occupation was moral *because it was legal.* To argue that it violated international law solves nothing. International law is as human, and subjective, as city fire codes and Third Reich decrees. Suppose the Nazis had conquered the world and in every land made laws that legalized the genocide? International law would not, then, have been violated, because the murder of the Jews would no longer be criminal anywhere. When no law is violated, no crime is committed.

If, as Sartre said, there is "no infinite and perfect consciousness to think" them, then there are no transcendent, transnational, and eternal moral values. How could there be? To talk about something "eternally moral," in this context, is like asking what happens a mile north of the North Pole, or at five degrees below absolute zero. It's meaningless. If there's no morality prior to, or independent of, human activity, then moral views are as human as body odor. Morals exist only because people (including Nazis) think them up, hew them out, and justify them along the way, which means people can read truths from panzer tracks as ancients read them from sheep livers. However extracted, morals rise no higher than the human, which rarely exceeds seven feet.

Suppose, too, that under their propaganda the Nazis convinced the whole world that murdering Jews was a moral necessity. What criteria—using all available resources in a secular, atheistic weltanschauung—could one draw from to dispute them? Can what the whole world thinks right be wrong? To argue that the genocide violates human nature doesn't work, because the Holocaust was central to the Nazi *moral* vision: The Jews, they believed, were blood-sucking vermin whose existence degraded human life and human nature everywhere. For the good of humanity, to best *preserve* human nature Jews had to be eradicated.

"Only what proves itself to every man and woman is so/Only what nobody denies is so,"[23] wrote Walt Whitman. But how do you prove the immorality of what nobody denies is moral?

You can't, unless there exists some ethical norm that transcends the human, something above culture and testosterone, a value system independent of what "proves itself to every man and woman," something eternal, unchanging . . . even, perhaps, divine?

---

[1] Albert Camus, *The Stranger* (New York: Vintage Books, 1988), p. 107.

[2] *Ibid.*, p. 122.

[3] Albert Camus, *The Myth of Sisyphus and Other Essays* (New York: Vintage Books, 1955), p. 68.

[4] Camus, *The Stranger,* p. 41.

[5] Steven Weinberg, *Dreams of a Final Theory* (New York: Vintage Books, 1992), p. 255.

[6] Laurens van der Post, *The Seed and the Sower* and *The Sword and the Doll* (New York: William Morrow, 1963), p. 115.

[7] Blaise Pascal, *Pensées* (New York: Penguin Books, 1995), p. 66.

[8] Walt Whitman, *Leaves of Grass* (New York: Penguin Books, 1986), p. 44.

[9] Friedrich Nietzsche, *Thus Spoke Zarathustra,* in *The Portable Nietzsche,* ed. Walter Kaufmann (New York: Viking Press, 1968), p. 125.

[10] *Ibid.*

[11] Nietzsche, *The Gay Science,* in *The Portable Nietsche,* p. 447.

[12] Nietzsche, *Thus Spoke Zarathustra,* p. 125.

[13] *Ibid.*

[14] *Ibid.,* p. 127.

[15] Nietzsche, *The Gay Science,* p. 125.

[16] Jean-Paul Sartre, *Existentialism and Human Emotions* (New York: Philosophical Library, 1957), p. 22.

[17] Bertrand Russell, *Human Society in Ethics and Politics* (New York: Mentor Books, 1962), p. 21.

[18] J. L. Mackie, *The Miracle of Theism* (Oxford: The Clarendon Press, 1982), p. 116.

[19] Fyodor Dostoyevsky, *The Brothers Karamazov* (New York: Oxford University Press, 1985), p. 675.

[20] Fyodor Dostoyevsky, *Crime and Punishment* (New York: Bantam Books, 1981), p. 63.

[21] *Ibid.,* p. 453.

[22] Sophocles, *Antigone* (New York: Dell, 1965), p. 43.

[23] Whitman, p. 54.

Chapter 2

Chemical Dilemma

leafless tree, a country road, and two homeless men vying for existence. It's night, and everything's shrouded in the bottom of the
earth's shadow. That's all it takes, the bottom of the shadow, and the
world goes half dark. Vladimir and Estragon wait, in the dark half, for a
mysterious figure whose promise to come prods them toward life.

"His name is Godot?" asks Estragon.

"I think so," answers Vladimir.[1]

As they stand, suckled by the dehydrated hope that Godot will come
(as promised), a procession of human suffering missteps, goose-steps,
limps, hobbles, and stomps past them. Bored not so much by all the pain
as by its uselessness, Estragon and Vladimir seek diversion in doing good,
such as lifting a blind man who has stumbled.

"Come, let's get to work!" says Vladimir. "In an instant all will vanish and we'll be alone once more, in the midst of nothingness!"[2] But as
Vladimir reaches, he falls and can't get up.

Despite more promises that Godot will come, they lean toward death,
again—this time planning to hang themselves. Having no rope, Estragon
takes off the cord that holds up his pants, which collapse around his an-
kles. Testing the cord's strength, they pull; it breaks, and both men almost
fall. They decide to find a better rope, and try again . . . later.

"We'll hang ourselves tomorrow," says Vladimir. "Unless Godot
comes."

"And if he comes?" asks Estragon.

"We'll be saved."[3]

Godot, of course, never comes; which means they're never saved. Of
course, they were never meant to be—which is why, from its first perfor-
mance at Paris's Théâtre de Babylone in 1953, Samuel Beckett's drama
Waiting for Godot always ends with these two atrophied souls stranded in an
existence they hate but can't escape. Nor were they even sure they should

19

try, because they had the promise, the promise Godot would come. That Godot never arrives hardly matters; what matters is the promise that he will.

Though only slashes, dots, and swirls besmirched (originally in French) strips of desiccated forest, the words of Beckett's popular drama have coalesced into the most merciless and cruel anti-Christian polemic since Voltaire's acid invective sizzled holes in the pews of eighteenth-century European cathedrals right out from under the pious derrieres that warmed them every Sunday. It's hard to imagine serious Christians who believe in the Second Coming not seeing themselves caricatured, to some degree, in Vladimir and Estragon's pathetic attempt to balance their fears and doubts about the absurd suffering that unfurls wherever human flesh and spirit converge with a loving and all-powerful God, who has promised to come and roll it all back and make it all right—but hasn't.

The apostle Peter, in the New Testament, predicted that "in the last days scoffers, walking after their own lusts" would say, "Where is the promise of his coming? for since the fathers fell asleep, all things continue as they were from the beginning of the creation" (2 Peter 3:3, 4). *Well, Peter, according to your contemporary, John, Jesus did promise to "come quickly" (Revelation 22:20), and that was about . . . 1,900 years ago. And after all those centuries, things are kind of, well, continuing "as they were." Thus, to be fair, Peter, the scoffers do—it would seem—have a point.* Peter and John probably never imagined something so far away as 1953. Beckett didn't have to imagine it; he was there.

Beckett's tragicomedy in two acts didn't mock just the promise, but also life without the promise, the promise of something beyond the earth and the conditionality of its gifts (for what the earth gives it *always* takes back). What's worse, Beckett asks, a (possibly) false hope, or no hope at all?

However unkind to the Second Coming, *Waiting for Godot* was worse to the secularist. It ruthlessly brutalized the heart whose dull tom-tom beats like a morose bureaucracy that exists only to keep itself alive. As the drama mimicked and mimed the obtuse mimicry and empty mimes of lives performed without final purpose, Beckett asks the question that has deflowered every quiet, reflective moment of the post-Christian world: How does one live a life that has no meaning?

Asininely, as the pathetic characters in *Waiting for Godot* reveal. Life is too complicated, too complex, too full of traps and inexplicable twists and unexpected tricks, to be lived—in and of itself—any other way. When people have no clue to the purpose of their existence, when they frame only diluted hypotheses about their origins, when all they can do is speculate—grossly at that—on what death brings (logically, the most important question of all, because whatever follows death will, no doubt, last *a lot* longer than the life that preceded it), then it's a wonder that humans live even as well as asininely.

"I do not know who put me into the world," wrote Pascal (putting himself in the mind of a skeptic), "nor what the world is, nor what I am myself. I am terribly ignorant about everything. I do not know what my body is, or my senses, or my soul, or even that part of me which thinks what I am saying, which reflects upon everything and about itself, and does not know itself any better than it knows anything else. I see the terrifying spaces of the universe hemming me in, and I find myself attached to one corner of this vast expanse without knowing why I have been put in this place rather than that, or why the brief span of life allotted to me should be assigned to one moment rather than another of all the eternity which went before me and all that will come after me. I see only infinity on every side, hemming me in like an atom or like the shadow of a fleeting instant. All I know is that I must soon die, but what I know least about is this very death which I cannot evade."[4]

Not exactly a formula for a full, happy, and meaningful existence, yet it's all that human life—in and of itself, lived only for itself—can extract from itself. "We can neither," wrote Francisco José Moreno, "rid ourselves of the certainty of death nor achieve an understanding of life."[5] How incredible that something so basic, so fundamental, as life can't even justify, much less explain its own existence!

Most births aren't annunciated by a bright chorus of heavenly beings. We don't come with instructions, explanations, or justifications written within the folds of our baby fat or decoded from our most primeval cries. We just, one day, are born. Eventually we become aware of ourselves—pain, fear, hunger often being the first sensations of self-consciousness. Uninvited, life is foisted upon those who never asked for it, yet remains difficult to give back if we don't want it and impossible to retain if we do. We're given something none sought after, planned for, or acquiesced in; we're not sure what it is, what it means, or even why we have it; its most real and immediate givens—pain, sorrow, loss, fear—remain inexplicable. Nevertheless, we cling to it fervently, passionately, and instinctively, even though without exception—and often after a miserable, bitter, and fruitless battle—we lose it anyway.

Is this human life (or a hopelessly gangrenous limb)?

Waiting for Godot divided reality into two spheres—one was mechanistic and atheistic and secular, in which irreducible truths exist only as mathematical equations on the upside of down quarks and resonate through the amoral symmetry of superstring reality; the other a spiritual dimension that transcended a single-tiered existence and proclaimed that irreducible truth doesn't originate in the creation but in the Creator. In the first sphere, humanity's the means, the ends, the one in whom it all culminates and climaxes; in the second, God is. In the first, humanity is the subject of truth; in the second, it's the object, and a vast gulf exists between the two.

The divide isn't some twentieth-century question. "We answer," wrote Aristotle, "that if there is no substance other than those which are formed by nature, natural science will be the first science; but if there is an immovable substance [his famous Unmoved Mover], the science of this must be prior and must be first philosophy, and universal in this way, because it is first."[6]

If the mechanistic, atheistic option is true, then our responses in the long run don't really matter; the end's the same for all, regardless of who they are or what they think, believe, or ever do. If the second is true, our responses are cradled with the weight of eternity. If the first is true, we'll never know; only the second offers the indubitable hope of absolutes.

Between these two centers of gravity a black fog looms. The option of a compromise, of a balance, of some Hegelian synthesis between them at "the end of history," doesn't (ultimately) and can't (logically) exist. There's an impassable distance between Athens and Jerusalem. It's either one or the other, but not both—even if both come heavily mortgaged with their own presuppositions, their own epistemological subterfuge, and their own leaps of faith beyond raw, hard-boned logic. Neither view's epistemic architecture is so tightly woven, so perfectly packaged and finely aligned, that even their most faithful adherents can't trip over the loose ends or thud against the rough edges. No matter how tightly fused to one's beliefs or what snug justification exists for them, they are still *only* beliefs—subjective encounters with phenomena, mere opinions always tainted by what was woven in the genes at conception or by what's frothing in the belly at the moment of thought.

Belief, ultimately, has no bearing upon the truth or the falsity of its object. No matter how fervent, pandemic, or incorrigible, belief can't make the false true or the true false. What's false never existed, even when we passionately believed that it did; the truth, in contrast, remains true long after we stopped believing in it.

With his five unenviable characters on a barren stage, Samuel Beckett dramatized the West's most immediate dilemma: God is dead, so where does that leave those made in His image? For Beckett, they're left between two hard fetters: (1) Christ hasn't come and (2) our sad lot because He hasn't. Between these cruel fates, humanity's manacled in a bond that offers no escape. How could it, when the knot itself is made of all reality, when it's woven of the only options possible, and when it's tied together by irreducible logic?

"Nothing to be done," mutters Estragon.[7] There's nothing *to do* because, frankly, nothing *can* be done—not in a godless universe where our most inflexible and uncompromising enemy accepts no surrender and takes no prisoners, but strafes, snipes, and shells until every cell wall crumbles and all within drains out and decays. Death is a foe impossible for us to hunt out and destroy because it's made out of what we are. In a naturalistic single-tiered universe, what is life and what is death but different mixes of the same stew? The living are just a pubescent version of the dead.

From the pre-Socratic Protagoras, who said, "As to the gods, I have no means of knowing either that they exist or that they do not exist. For many are the obstacles that impede knowledge, both the obscurity of the question and the shortness of human life,"[8] up through the a priori materialistic presuppositions of modern science—a spiritless, naturalistic worldview has had a long (in that it stretches way back) but thin (in that few adhered to it) history.

Out of thousands of years, only during the past 100 (fewer, actually) has the flimsily thin but thickly insular perspective of secularism tilted the whole edifice of Western thought, which its cultural, scientific, and intellectual literati have preached with the fervor of crusaders pillaging, raping, and plundering their way to the Holy Land. Conceived in the debris of the seventeenth-century Cromwellian revolution, birthed in arable Enlightenment ideals, breast-fed by the goddess of reason, schooled in

Parisian *salons,* and unwittingly encouraged—even justified—by those arrayed in the numinous garb of Christ but who have cast the shadows of cold dark angels instead, secularism matured only in the twentieth century, where it's so infused into Western culture we'd have to climb out of our eyes in order to see what it has done to our minds.

For hundreds of years people slit each other's throats because they couldn't agree on what God did to them after their throats were slit. Today, for so many people in such a systematic, calculated, and scientific manner to argue that there is no God who does anything to us (either before or after we slit each other's throats), and even to shift the chassis of an entire civilization on that premise, represents a radical change. Never before has there been such a widespread, institutionalized, and intellectually fertile movement to explain creation and all its predicates (life, death, morals, law, purpose, love, whatever)—without a Creator.

Why bother with the texts of the dead when there's the scientism of the living? What can Jeremiah, Isaiah, and Paul possibly say to those raised on Newton, Einstein, and Heisenberg? Didn't the *Principia* vitiate the Apocalypse? Who needs the Lord moving over the "face of the waters" (Genesis 1:2) when Darwin did the same on the H.M.S. *Beagle?*

Wrapped in airtight numbers (as opposed to scoreless psalms), expressed by scientists (not dead prophets), and explained by universally testable theories (not unverifiable stories from vanquished cultures), the secular worldview has commanded an aura of objectivity, of validation, and of demonstration that's (at least for now) beyond the reach of religious faith. Special relativity has enjoyed proofs that Christ's death and resurrection haven't.

Arthur Stanley Eddington, on May 29, 1919, could point a telescope toward an eclipse and prove that gravity does (as theorized) bend light. Nothing, however, has been pointed in the heavens, in the earth, or in any direction that has proved, with such verifiable and empirical objectivity, that Christ is the Son of God who at the cross shed His blood as an atonement for sin. People need faith to believe that "in a moment, in the twinkling of an eye, at the last trump: for the trumpet shall sound, and the dead shall be raised incorruptible" (1 Corinthians 15:52) or that "God commendeth his love toward us, in that, while we were yet sinners, Christ died for us" (Romans 5:8), but not that "for every action there is an equal and opposite reaction" or that the force of gravity between two objects is inversely proportional to the square of the distance between their centers of gravity.

Numbers (particularly those queued in formulas) come garbed with an inherent stability, a focus, a permanency that words, fluctuating, grainy, and moody (however queued), can never wear. Fledgling, relatively short-lived, and parochial, the materialistic scientific worldview has, nevertheless, harnessed the moment even if its Potemkin tethers have proved not only inadequate but have also tied the time with knots slowly unraveling through the momentum of their own slipshod and shabby loops.

Indeed, despite paeans to the triumph of scientific rationalism, its victory has never been joined to anything except itself and its own dogmatic presuppositions. The fit, in fact, is not as tight has been taught, and the longer it shrouds the world, the more threadbare the cover becomes, until reality is bursting through the seams. Sure, the world flashes across our senses as material; sure, rational thinking solves puzzles and helps jets fly; sure, science has dissected the atom and constructed the space shuttle. Yet these facts don't prove that materialism, rationalism, and science contain the potential—or even the tools—to explain all reality any more than classical physics alone explains France's 1998 World Cup victory.

There's something about Tennyson's *Enoch Arden* or Lord Byron's *Don Juan* that accesses a dimension in which science is too bulky, too crude, too broad to enter, a dimension in which reason is too staid, too hard, too inflexible to pass through. Cold, dead, static equations inadequately define a reality riotous with passion, effusive with thought, and spry with creativity. What algorithm can explain the passion of *King Lear,* what formula the cooing of a dove, what law the foreboding of Van Gogh's *Wheatfield With Crows?* Theories and formulas, principles and laws, don't make stars shine, robins fly, or mothers feed their young any more than carving the symbols $E = mc^2$ on a piece of refined uranium will make an atomic explosion.

However great the scientific achievements of the past few hundred years, something primal, something essential and intrinsically human has been squandered along the way. Between Isaac Newton's "O God! I think thy thoughts after thee!" and Stephen Hawking's (who occupies the same chair at Cambridge that Newton did) "The human race is just a chemical scum on a moderate-sized planet, orbiting around a very average star in the outer suburb of one among hundreds of billion of galaxies"[9] a whole dimension, unable to fit in test tubes or conform to formulas, has been written out of nature, demoted from reality to myth, shifted from the world to the mind. In this new calculus, heaven—instead of being the throne of the cosmos—has been shattered, the pieces parceled out and fragmented into nothing but fickle myths scattered in the human imagination. And the God who once reigned in that heaven now, instead, cowers—twice removed from that throne (created by the creatures He had once created).

Yet not just the divine has been contorted and demoted in order to fit the frame that for the past hundred years has outlined the boundaries of all reality. Whole aspects of human existence have been painfully crammed by scientific rationalism and materialism into containers that hold them no better than cigar boxes can the scent of angels. Ethics and love, hate and hope, transcend not just the periodic table of elements but all 112 other facets of reality that the table represents. Np, Am, Ar, Kr, Xe, Os, Re, Tc, Cs, Ba, Si, and the 101 rest—no matter how microscopically finely tuned and balanced the proportions—can't fully explain heroism, art, fear, generosity, altruism, hate, hope, and passion. To pretend that they can is to equate Luciano Pavarotti singing *Il Barbiere di Siviglia* with belching.

A worldview that limits its world, and its view, only to rationalism, to materialism, and to scientific atheism misses all that's beyond them—which is so much of us, of what we are, of what we hope for, of what we aspire to, of what we imagine, of what we dream and laugh and cry about and love and worship and live and die for. Chemical scum doesn't mull over loftier worlds, doesn't envision eternity, doesn't write *Hamlet,* doesn't weep for the pain of others, doesn't evoke the sublime, doesn't desire immortality, doesn't seek the Good, and doesn't love (either conditionally or unconditionally). That formulas and chemicals are part of it, of course; that they are all of it, of course not—and to think that they are is to surrender oneself to the lowest and cheapest denominator.

In fact, in a purely materialistic chemical and mechanical world, how can humans be morally responsible? If physical laws alone control us, we're like the wind, or combustion. Any society based on purely materialistic premises must let its murderers, child molesters, thieves, rapists, and all other offenders go free because we're machines, and who can ascribe moral culpability to a gizmo? It would be like putting an Uzi on trial for murder. No society, even those glossed with secularism, allows for such moral inculpability, except among the insane. Thus, what society says—implicitly, at least—is that if scientific materialism were true, we'd all have to be lunatics.

Every culture, every society, rejects hardcore materialism, believing instead that we're morally responsible beings not manipulated by deterministic physical forces beyond our control. We're animated, obviously, by something more than what we immediately perceive—even if we don't know what, or how it works, but only that it's there and real and without it we're not alive, not free, not human.

Kant argued that the mere act of reason itself surpasses nature, transcends emotions, trumps urges, and upstages instincts. How, too, could we even think transcendent thoughts if there were not something about us beyond nature, something greater than the sum of our chemicals, something more to our minds than soggy, pulsating meat? Can effects be greater than their causes? Can molecules alone, no matter how complicated, think, love, and fear? Are Flaubert's *Madame Bovary* and Augustine's *Confessions* nothing but chemical reactions? Isn't there more to imagination than quanta of neurotransmitters lunging across synaptic clefts? Otherwise, what does the brain do, secrete ideas like the liver does bile?

We're not glorified rocks; the Hope Diamond is, but not us. Mud, no matter how carefully crafted and coiffed, can't make a daffodil, a passionate thought, a child's laugh. Ten thousand pieces of glittering glass—no matter how sharply cut, intricately designed, or finely fused—can't make a butterfly dance on the wind; they can't make the dance, not even the wind. They can't make a butterfly rotting on a leaf, not the rotting, not even the leaf. All combinations, proportions, and melding of everything that science, rationalism, and materialism say that we are never can make us heroes or lovers, but because some of us are—science, rationalism, and materialism are not broad, liberated, and imaginative enough to encompass the world, much less the human spirit, despite its grandiose claims to the contrary.

"What science cannot tell us," Bertrand Russell once told a BBC audience, "mankind cannot know."[10]

Really? Then we can't know love, we can't know hate, we can't know mercy, we can't know good or evil or happiness or art or transcendence or faith, or at least we can't know them as anything other than versions of indigestion, high cholesterol, and bunions. But because *we do* know them as something more, something greater, something more sublime, a worldview like scientific materialism, which says we *can't,* is obviously inadequate, for it makes us nothing more than the monster in Mary Shelley's *Frankenstein,* "man" created by human means alone.

Wrote mathematician David Berlinksi, "An uneasy sense nonetheless prevails—it has *long* prevailed—that the vision of a purely physical or material universe is somehow incomplete; it cannot encompass the familiar but inescapable facts of ordinary life."[11]

Scientism and materialism can't even justify themselves or their own existence, much less explain everything else's. Austrian mathematician Kurt Gödel showed that no system of thought, even scientific, can be legitimized by anything within the system itself. You have to step outside the system, to view it from a different, grander, and broader perspective in order to appraise it. Otherwise, how does one judge x, when x itself is the very criterion used to do the judging? How can humans objectively study the act of thinking when they have only the act of thinking with which to do it? It would be easier to take off your shoes while jogging.

For hundreds of years reason has reigned as epistemological king of the Occident, the sole criterion for judging truth, the monarch whose word was often deemed dogma, creed, and law. Yet what has been the criterion for judging reason? Reason itself, of course! After all, what else can one use to judge reason but reason itself? Yet to judge reason by reason is like defining a word by using the word itself in the definition. It's a tautology, and tautologies prove little or nothing. How fascinating, then, that reason itself—the foundation of thought, particularly, of modern thought—can't be validated.

The problem for scientism and materialism is How can one step outside a system, into a wider frame of reference, when the system itself purports to encompass all reality? What happens when we reach the edge of the universe? What's beyond it? If there were a wider frame of reference to judge it from (God, perhaps?), then the system itself would not be all-encompassing, as scientific materialism often claims to be.

"In short," wrote scientist Timothy Ferris, "there is not and will never be a complete and comprehensive scientific account of the universe that can be proved valid."[12] In other words, even science and materialism will always have to be taken on . . . faith.

What? Could it be that the inherent limits of science itself require faith? But isn't faith, the notion of belief in something improvable, outside the purview of science, whose whole purpose is to prove things empirically? Isn't the concept of faith a leftover from a distant, mythic pre-rationalistic, pre-scientific age?

Because science is based on materialism, science implies (at least hypothetically) that everything should be accessible to experiment and empirical validation. Ideally, there shouldn't be room for faith in a scientific, secular, materialistic universe, *yet the very nature of that universe demands it.* What a paradox! The same system that verbally refutes faith inherently implies it. Within the materialistic and scientific worldview, then, there reigns the potential for something beyond it, something outside of it, something that explains why love is more than endocrines, ethics more than physics, and beauty more than math. Something, perhaps . . . divine?

---

[1] Samuel Beckett, *Waiting for Godot* (New York: Grove Press, 1982), p. 17.

[2] *Ibid.,* p. 92.

[3] *Ibid.,* p. 109.

[4] Blaise Pascal, *Pensées,* p. 130.

[5] Francisco José Moreno, *Between Faith and Reason* (New York: Harper Colophon Books, 1977), p. 7.

[6] *Aristotle: Selections,* ed. W. D. Ross (New York: Charles Scribner's Sons, 1955), p. 63.

[7] Beckett. p. 17.

[8] *From Thales to Plato,* ed. T. V. Smith (Chicago: University of Chicago Press, 1956), p. 60.

[9] Quoted in David Deutsch, *The Fabric of Reality* (New York: Penguin Books, 1997), pp. 177, 178.

[10] Quoted in Ted Peters, "Science and Theology: Where Are We?" *Journal of Science and Religion,* 31, no. 2 (June 1996). See www.templeton.org/science/jun962.asp.

[11] David Berlinski, *The Advent of the Algorithm* (New York: Harcourt, 2000), pp. 249, 250.

[12] Timothy Ferris, *Coming of Age in the Milky Way* (New York: Doubleday, 1988), p. 384.

[Chapter 3]

Quantum Leaps

I was in search of an answer to my question," wrote Tolstoy (via Constantin Levin in *Anna Karenin*). "But reason could not give an answer to my question—reason is incommensurable with the problem. The answer has been given by life itself, through my knowledge of what is right and what is wrong. And this knowledge I did not acquire in any way: it was given to me as it is to everybody—*given,* because I could not have got it from anywhere.

"Where did I get it from? Would reason ever have proved to me that I must love my neighbour instead of strangling him? I was told that in my childhood, and I believed it gladly, for they told me what was already in my soul. But who discovered it? Not reason. Reason discovered the struggle for existence, and the law demanding that I should strangle all who hinder the satisfaction of my desires. That is the deduction of reason. But loving one's neighbour reason could never discover, because it's unreasonable."[1]

Loving one's neighbor isn't the half of it, either. According to the Gospel writer John, after Lazarus had died and was buried in a cave sealed with a stone, "Jesus said, 'Take away the stone.' Martha, the sister of the dead man, said to him, 'Lord, by this time there will be an odor, for he has been dead four days.' Jesus said to her, 'Did I not tell you that if you would believe you would see the glory of God?' So they took away the stone. And Jesus lifted up his eyes and said, 'Father, I thank thee that thou hast heard me. I knew that thou hearest me always, but I have said this on account of the people standing by, that they may believe that thou didst send me.' When he had said this, he cried with a loud voice, 'Lazarus, come out.' The dead man came out, his hands and feet bound with bandages, and his face wrapped with a cloth. Jesus said to them, 'Unbind him, and let him go'" (John 11:39-44, RSV).

In his Gospel, Luke says that when Jesus "was in one of the cities, there came a man full of leprosy; and when he saw Jesus, he fell on his face and besought him, 'Lord, if you will, you can make me clean.' And he stretched out his hand, and touched him, saying, 'I will; be clean.' And immediately the leprosy left him" (Luke 5:12, 13, RSV).

Mark recounts a night on the Sea of Galilee with Jesus. "And leaving the crowd, they took him with them in the boat, just as he was. And other boats were with him. And a great storm of wind arose, and the waves beat into the boat, so that the boat was already filling. But he was in the stern, asleep on the cushion; and they woke him and said to him, 'Teacher, do you not care if we perish?' And he awoke and rebuked the wind, and said to the sea, 'Peace! Be still!' And the wind ceased, and there was a great calm. He said to them, 'Why are you afraid? Have you no faith?' And they were filled with awe, and said to one another, 'Who then is this, that even wind and sea obey him?'" (Mark 4:36-41, RSV).

After Peter (in Matthew's Gospel) had been asked about whether his Master paid the Temple tax, Jesus said to the fisherman: "Go thou to the sea, and cast an hook, and take up the fish that first cometh up; and when thou hast opened his mouth, thou shalt find a piece of money: that take, and give unto them for me and thee" (Matthew 17:27).

Four different incidents, expressed by four different writers, yet in each one Jesus revealed what Constantin Levin learned—that truth is richer, deeper, and more resplendent than reason alone allows and that to limit one's concept of reality to reason is like limiting one's concept of music to bongo drums. By His words (and more so by His deeds), Jesus exposed vistas far beyond the epistemological bigotry of common sense, uncovered realms in which logic and reason are as useful as sign language among the dead, and unfurled dimensions not only greater than our axioms but that with infinite jest scorn their naïveté and corny finality.

For the past century, though, physics has been doing the same thing, only less mercifully than Jesus did—repealing our most fundamental and reasonable assumptions about reality. Few things, if any, that Jesus said or did have heaped the kind of intellectual snubs and cerebral rebuffs upon our concepts of logic, reason, and reality that relativity (general and special), quantum physics, and super string theory have during the past 100 years. In contrast to the natural world, the world of relative time, of quarks, of curved space, of matter waves, of 10-dimensional universes, of Heisenberg's uncertainty principle, of nonlocality, of the double-slit experiment, of probability-waves, of WIMPs, of neutrinos, and of the many worlds interpretation—the supernatural realm (the realm that Jesus uniquely revealed) seems all but intuitive, if not easily believable, by comparison.

Consider quantum theory, one of the most demonstrated, studied, and applied branches of modern physics. "Quantum theory," wrote physicist Paul Davies, "is primarily a practical branch of physics, and as such is brilliantly successful. It has given us the laser, the electron microscope, the transistor, the superconductor, and nuclear power. At a stroke it explained chemical bonding, the structure of the atom and nucleus, the conduction of electricity, the mechanical and thermal properties of solids, the stiffness of collapsed stars, and a host of other important physical phenomena. . . . In short, the quantum theory is, in its everyday application, a very down-to-earth subject with a vast body of supporting evidence, not only from commercial gadgetry, but from careful and delicate scientific experiments."[2]

The question is not whether quantum physics is real or if it works; it definitely is and definitely does. The question, instead, is Why does quantum physics not only shatter the image that humanity has had of the world for centuries but also put the pieces back into a picture so weird that our minds haven't yet devised a language to explain it?

Few things, for instance, expose the opacity of the human more than the famous double-slit quantum experiment. A pebble dropped in a pool of water makes rings of waves. If going through two holes in a barrier bordering more water, the waves make smaller wave patterns on the other side of each hole. If both holes are near enough to each other, the smaller sets of waves coming out of the holes merge and create a distinct interference pattern in the water on the other side of the barrier.

Beams of light going through two holes in a barrier do, basically, the same thing. They make small waves, and (if the holes are close enough) the waves meet outside the holes and, like water, create a typical wave interference pattern (in this case on a photographic plate) beyond the barrier. This interference pattern appears as a series of light and dark lines, like stripes.

Besides beams of light, individual photons, one at a time, can be sent through the holes as well. If one hole (or slit) is closed, and one photon at a time is shot through the other, the photons merely pile up on the other side of the hole, much like rocks thrown one at a time through a hole in a wall. If, while rocks are being thrown through one hole, another hole is made in the wall beyond the trajectory of the thrown rocks, the second hole would make no difference in what happened at the first one. The rocks merely continue to pile up behind the first, regardless of the second.

Now the tricky part. If photons are being shot one at a time through the first hole, and a second hole is opened (out of the trajectory of the photons), the second hole should make no difference about what happens at the first one. The photons, like the rocks, should simply continue to pile up outside the first hole. Right?

Wrong! If, as the photons are shot one by one through the first hole, a second hole is opened, a wave interference pattern forms on the other side of the barrier! The same pattern appears that would occur if beams of light were going through both holes, creating their own waves and then mixing together, making a wave interference pattern. But they're not; only one photon at a time is being shot through one hole. It's as if, while rocks were being thrown only through the first hole, they started to pile up outside the second as well!

Again, the individual photons are being fired, just as before, one at a time through the first hole. Nothing has changed except the appearance of the second hole, which—from a purely common sense, logical, and reasonable perspective—should make no more difference here, with photons, than it would with the rocks. The photons, like the rocks, should simply pile up outside the hole they're being shot through, regardless of the other hole. But that's not what happens; instead, once a second hole is opened, the photons make a wave pattern—a series of light and dark lines—on the other side of the barrier, a rather bizarre and inexplicable fact about the nature of reality.

First, how did the photons "know" (if that's even the right word) that the second hole had been opened? How could a photon, in and of itself (a presumably "not-conscious" entity), be "aware" of the second hole, and then respond to it? "It also appears," wrote Gary Zukav in his book *The Dancing Wu Li Masters,* "that the photons in the double-split experiment somehow 'know' whether or not both slits are open and that they act accordingly."[3]

Somehow, and no one knows how (though physicists have ventured some incredible guesses), the photons can "tell" that the second hole is open.

Next, once it "knows" about the second hole, how does a single photon "split" (again, if that's the right word), find the second hole, and go through it (and through the first hole) at the same time (if that is what, in fact, it does)?

And, finally, how does the photon know where to place itself in the overall interference pattern? How does it know that, because of the second hole, it has to reach the photographic plate on the other side like a wave? Somehow the photon not only has to know the second hole was opened and then get through it (along with the first one), but then it also has to arrange itself on the photographic plate in a wave interference pattern.

"Although each photon starts out as a particle," wrote astrophysicist John Gribbin, "and arrives as a particle, it seems to have gone through both holes at once, interfered with itself, and worked out just where to place itself on the film to make its own minute contribution to the overall interference pattern. The behaviour encompasses two mysteries. First, how does the single photon go through both holes at once? Secondly, even if it does perform this trick, how does it 'know' where to place itself in the overall pattern? Why doesn't every photon follow the same trajectory and end up in the same spot on the other side?"[4]

The double-split experiment, giving common sense all the certitude of a mad dog's dream (photons can't be "aware" of anything, much less how many holes are in a wall!) leads into what physicists call nonlocality, another facet of the natural that makes the supernatural look banal, even boring, by comparison. ("Anyone who is not shocked by quantum theory," wrote quantum pioneer Niels Bohr, "has not understood it.")[5]

Two photons are released from an atom and separate. The distance between them doesn't matter. What matters, however, is that the moment the spin of one of the photons is observed (notice the term *observed),* the spin of the second one will immediately—at a speed faster than light—start to spin in the opposite direction. Imagine two cue balls, one in Belgrade, one in Sydney. The moment someone observes the spin of the one in Belgrade, the one in Sydney spins in the opposite direction!

But that's impossible. How can observing something change it? Even worse, how can observing one thing change something else, especially something so far away—and do it at a speed faster than light? (Hadn't Einstein proved that nothing, not even information, can travel faster than light?) Yet no matter how much it defies all that logic, reason, and our basic understanding of reality have told us for centuries about how the world works, nonlocality is an undeniable characteristic of the quantum realm, the realm upon which all that's physical is made. When a person observes one aspect of that realm, another aspect—regardless of the distance—is immediately changed. Looking at the cue ball in Belgrade changes the one in Sydney.

"This is quantum weirdness," wrote physics professor and author Timothy Ferris. "Interfering with one part of a quantum system alters the results observed in another part, even when the system has been enlarged to enormous dimensions. . . . It is as if the quantum world had never heard of space—as if, in some strange way, it thinks of itself as being in one place at a time."[6]

Ferris used the term *interfering*. By that he meant only "observing" or "measuring," nothing more—which leads to another aspect of the quantum world that makes the impossible indubitable, and this is known as the "Copenhagen interpretation," in which the subject-object barrier is broken down (if it even existed at all). In the quantum realm, a "thing" (not the best word) doesn't really "exist" (again, not an accurate word for this situation) until someone observes it; then, and only then, does it become "real" (another word inadequately describing quantum phenomena). Until observed—that is, until a person looks at or detects or measures it—this subatomic "entity" "exists" in a ghostlike state called a "wave function" that "collapses" into a particle after being observed or measured.

A coin, flat on a table, is either heads up or tails up, regardless of whether someone looks at it, right? When someone finally does look, one sees what was already there, either the heads up or the tails up, right? One's observation of the coin didn't determine which side was up. Right? Common sense. Right?

Wrong! At least at the quantum level. The "coin" (a subatomic "particle" such as a photon or electron) is neither heads up nor tails up. It "exists," rather, in a nebulous state until measured or observed. Only then, after being "seen" (another inadequate word), does it "collapse" into something "real" (either heads or tails). Until that measurement, or observation, it was a "wave function," or a "probability wave"—"something" that's "there" but not "real," something that "is" and yet at the same time "is not."

According to the Copenhagen interpretation, in the quantum realm the subject becomes—merely through the act of observation—intricately involved with the object, not the most intuitive intimation of reality. Common sense dictates the existence of the world and of things in the world as autonomous from one's observation of them. The tomb of Tutankhamen, though hidden from human sight for millennia, existed (one assumes) before being discovered by Howard Carter in 1922. Yet the notion of an objective reality, independent of observation, doesn't seem applicable at the most fundamental level of accessible matter. The question asked by the philosophes of idealism (the branch of philosophy which contends that reality's in the mind and nowhere else) about whether or not a tree that falls in the woods makes noise if no one hears it becomes, at least in the quantum world, more pertinent than those who first framed it could have (even in their most speculative moments of idealist whimsy) ever imagined.

As already noted, in the double-split experiment, when both holes are opened, a wave interference pattern forms on the other side of the barrier, even if photons are being shot, one at a time, through one hole. If, however, photon detectors at each hole detect which hole the photons go through, the wave interference pattern collapses and the photons pile up like rocks outside the first hole—just as they did when only that one hole was opened. The photons apparently "know" (again, what other word can one use?) that they are being detected and, as a result, the "wave function" (the state they appear to be in before detection) collapses and no wave pattern forms on the photographic plate. If a detector is placed at just one hole—even the second hole (though the photons are being directed through the first hole)—the "wave function" still collapses and the photons pile up outside the first hole. Somehow the photons going through the first hole "knew" (even before they got there) that someone was looking at the second hole and, as a result, behaved as particles, not waves. If both holes stayed open, but without a detector at either one—without anyone "looking"—a wave interference pattern again spreads out on the other side. Once detected, however, the wave pattern vanishes.

The Copenhagen interpretation is just one example of the incredible attempting to explain the inexplicable. There are others. According to the many-worlds interpretation, the universe is constantly splitting apart and making identical copies of itself except for the particular outcome of each quantum observation. In one universe, the quantum "coin" is heads, in another tails. Every time that a physicist looks to see whether a photon is a particle or a wave, the entire universe breaks off into a parallel clone. In each universe there's an identical lab, with identical equipment, with identical physicists, with identical suns, stars, moons, and galaxies. In one of these universes the physicist sees a wave, in the other a particle. Other than that single quantum difference, these parallel worlds are exact copies of each other. In fact, any time the universe is confronted with options at the quantum level, the universe splits into as many copies of itself as needed in order for every possible option at the subatomic level to be a reality, which means that untold trillions of parallel universes exist alongside our little slice of reality (hence the name many-worlds interpretation). However far-fetched this idea may sound, many physicists and cosmologists have accepted it (or various versions thereof) because, as one Oxford physicist said: "It is the explanation—the only one that is tenable—of a remarkable and counterintuitive reality."[7]

Irrational? Illogical? Unbelievable? Beyond common sense? Sounds like charges often leveled against Christianity, not science. But this isn't Christianity, religion, anything based on ancient authorities or divine revelation. This is science—indeed, modern physics, the excruciatingly specific study of physical phenomena, the empirically validated and mathematically based investigation of hard reality—and what it has yielded pulls and stretches and bends our brain in ways that make Christianity seem almost mathematical in contrast. It's arguably more "rational" to believe in what the apostle Paul has called the "foolishness" of the gospel than in what physicists have called the "absurdness" of quantum theory.

"There can be only one remedy," wrote physicist Roland Omnès regarding what quantum science has done to thought, and that is "to invent a new way of understanding."[8] That, or to accept that present ways of understanding are not quite broad enough to embrace the purely physical (much less the spiritual) aspects of reality. Writing about quantum reality, Omnès said: "This theory penetrates reality to a depth our senses cannot take us. Its laws are universal, and they rule over the world of objects so familiar to us. We, who inhabit the world, cannot make our own vision prevail over those arrogant laws, whose concepts seem to flow from an order higher than the one inspired by the things we can touch, see, and say with ordinary words."[9] Sounds almost like faith or religion, not science.

"But what appears certain," wrote physicist Brian Greene, "is that no matter how you interpret quantum mechanics, it undeniably shows that the universe is founded on principles that, from the standpoint of our day-to-day experiences, are bizarre."[10]

It's not just in the quantum realm—the realm of the super-small—that the physical outfoxes the mental. The macroscopic world, the world we're conscious of, the world we know, the world we see, feel, and intuit, does the same thing, only differently.

Take the notion of time, one of the "broadest" manifestations of reality. Time is the fourth dimension, united with height, width, and depth (space) into a single entity called "space-time." Time is (or at least appears to be) everywhere; all things we know about appear to exist within time. It's hard to imagine how anything—stars, galaxies, quasars, all that is—could not exist apart from time. Whatever time is, however it works, it's "big."

Now, if Martin is standing still and a train approaches him at 100 kilometers per hour, Martin and the train will meet at 100 kilometers per hour. If Martin runs toward the train at 20 kilometers per hour, Martin and the train will meet at 120 kilometers per hour. If Martin runs at 20 kilometers per hour in the same direction the train is moving, the train will pass him at 80 kilometers per hour. Pure classical physics, pure common sense, right?

If Martin is standing still and a beam of light approaches him at 300,000 kilometers per second (kps), it will reach him at 300,000 kps. If Martin moves toward that beam of light at 100,000 kps, then common sense, logic, and rational thinking—all the intellectual tools that proved cumbersome, even useless, in the quantum realm (like using a sledgehammer, axe, and mallet to fix a Pentium IV chip)—would dictate that the beam of light would reach him at . . . what? At 400,000 kps, what else? The light is moving at 300,000 kps, and Martin is moving toward it at 100,000 kps. So 100,000 plus 300,000 equals 400,000. Who needs an Einstein to figure that out?

Only one problem: the answer is wrong. The beam of light will still reach Martin (even when he's moving toward it at 100,000 kps) at 300,000 kps. If he is moving at 299,000 kps either toward the light or

299,000 kps away from it, there's no difference. The light will reach him always—no matter his speed relative to it—at the same rate, 300,000 kps.

But that's impossible. If Martin moves toward or away from something that is moving in his direction, the speed at which he meets it is relative to the speed at which he is moving either toward or away from it. That's pure common sense, that's pure logic, that's pure reason—and that is, of course, the problem. Reality (at least at the speed of light) doesn't correlate to logic, reason, or common sense any better than do photons and electrons. Instead, reality reveals that whenever anyone takes a measurement of the velocity of light, the light will always reach that person at the same rate, regardless of that person's constant motion relative to the light. Light moves 300,000 kps relative to anyone in a uniform frame of reference. No matter how fast you are steadily moving relative to a beam of light, that beam will reach you always at the same speed.

How could that be? The answer, formulated by Albert Einstein in 1905 and later verified with awesome accuracy by experiment, is so blatantly simple and patently obvious and overtly easy that it's utterly amazing not everyone 8 years old and upward automatically and intuitively grasped it from antiquity. Time slows down the faster one moves, and it does so in a proportional manner that always makes light approach its target at 300,000 kps, regardless of the uniform motion of whoever is observing or measuring it. Though Martin is moving at 100,000 kps toward the beam of light, a second for him (at his speed) slows down enough to ensure that the beam of light will reach him at 300,000 kps.

Actually, it's even simpler than this, for not only does time slow down, but any measuring rod or device used to measure the light shrinks in proportion to one's speed as well, ensuring the constancy of light's velocity in one's frame of reference. If Martin moved faster, time would slow down more and his measuring rod would shrink more—but just enough to ensure that the light would reach him at 300,000 kps.

This change isn't in the clock, as if speed did something to the gears, cranks, and dials. Time itself, and thus all that happens within time—such as the functions of Martin's brain, the beat of his heart, the flow of oxygen to his lungs, the blink of his eye, and the tick of his watch—slows down because time itself has slowed down. For Martin, nothing is different, everything is normal—everything is slowing down in exact proportion with everything else because time itself, as it relates to him in his frame of reference, is slowing down. To a person standing still who could watch Martin in motion, it would seem (to this person) that all Martin does (his movements, his speech, even the tick of his watch) is sluggish, slow, because for the other person time—the time that person exists in (as opposed to the time that Martin exists in)—is moving faster than it does for Martin.

This phenomenon, called the special theory of relativity, shows that nature at a fundamental level (time and light) pummels logic, reason, and common sense—the tools upon which humans have built most of their modern epistemic structures, proof of just how bumbling these structures can be. The point is not that logic or reason should be denied; they can't. (To do so would be to refute your own denial, because what would one be refuting logic or reason with other than logic or reason?) Instead, using logic, reason, and common sense, we look at the double-split experiment, at nonlocality, at special relativity, and from these simply recognize the limits of logic, reason, and common sense, that's all.

Of course, special relativity, nonlocality, and the double-split experiment don't prove the validity of religious faith; they weren't meant to, nor could they even if they were. Faith, like mathematical axioms, by definition exists outside "proof." If proved, they wouldn't be faith or axioms. What quantum theory and relativity show, instead, is that reality itself transcends logic, reason, and common sense much the way religion does. So to limit one's epistemic boundaries to logic, reason, and common sense is to look through a peephole and think you've found the edge of universe when instead all that's in your eye is an image of the front porch—in fact, only part of it, and even that's distorted. If the fundamental stuff of nature—the basic building blocks of all materiality—can so deftly evade the reach of reason, how foolish to dismiss outright faith on the same grounds. One might as well deny the existence of the material world. (Some folk, in fact, do.)

Twentieth-century science, far from squeezing out faith, has stretched reality so far and in so many diffuse directions that it has made more, not less, room for faith. If, as Hegel said, only the real is rational and only the rational real, then we need to radically redefine "real" or "rational," because for now (as the double-split experiment proves) the real is hardly "rational." What's more "rational": Jesus raising Lazarus from the dead, or photons "knowing" that the second hole is open?

One might, of course, find valid reasons to reject religious faith, but to do so in the age of quantum physics because it's unreasonable is, itself, unreasonable. You might as well reject special relativity because reason, logic, and common sense make it plain that time isn't elastic, that it can't be stretched or squeezed but always remains the same no matter how fast one is moving. Baffled by the mysterious phenomena of the super-small, befuddled by the "spooky action" (to quote Einstein) of nonlocality, and empirically challenged by the elasticity of time, for anyone to reject religious faith a priori on the premise that it's not rational is to practice a rather decrepit form of intellectual bigotry.

Years ago Werner Heisenberg, one of the founders of quantum physics, musing about the early days of this science, wrote: "I remember discussions with [Niels] Bohr which went through many hours very late at night and ended almost in despair; and when at the end of the discussion I went alone for a walk in the neighboring park I repeated to myself again and again the question: Can nature really be as absurd as it seems to us in these atomic experiments?"[11]

Perhaps he should have studied something a little more logical, a little more rational . . . like faith!

---

[1] Leo Tolstoy, *Anna Karenin* (New York: Penguin Books, 1978), p. 832.

[2] Paul Davies, *God and the New Physics* (New York: Touchstone Books, 1983), p. 101.

[3] Gary Zukav, *The Dancing Wu Li Masters* (New York: Bantam Books, 1980), p. 63.

[4] John Gribbin, *Schrödinger's Kittens and the Search for Reality* (New York: Little, Brown, and Company, 1995), p. 5.

[5] Quoted in Davies, p. 100.

[6] Timothy Ferris, *The Whole Shebang* (New York: Simon and Schuster, 1997), p. 267.

[7] David Deutsch, *The Fabric of Reality,* p. 51.

[8] Roland Omnès, *Quantum Philosophy* (Princeton, N.J.: Princeton University Press, 1999), p. 82.

[9] *Ibid.,* p. 163.

[10] Brian Greene, *The Elegant Universe* (New York: Vintage Books, 2000), p. 108.

[11] Werner Heisenberg, *Physics and Philosophy* (Amherst, N.Y.: Prometheus Books, 1999), p. 42.

[Chapter 4]

"The Children . . . What Am I to Do About Them?"

In one of the most finely tuned and tightly wrenched polemics against the God of Christian tradition, socialist Ivan Karamazov (in Dostoyevsky's book *The Brothers Karamazov)* told his brother, a monk, about a "serf-boy, a little child of eight," who—while playing with a stone—accidentally hurt the paw of a wealthy general's hound.

According to Ivan, the general (and owner of the land where the serf-boy lived) asked, "Why is my favorite dog lame?" When told, he had the boy taken outside and stripped naked before the general, his servants, his dog-boys, his hounds, his huntsmen, and the child's mother.

"He shivers," continued Ivan, "numb with terror, not daring to cry. . . . 'Make him run,' commands the general. 'Run! Run!' shout the dog-boys. The boy runs. . . . 'At him!' yells the general, and he sets the whole pack of hounds on the child. The hounds catch him, and tear him to pieces before his mother's eyes!"[1]

Ivan's point, in this tragic account—and the one about the Turks in Bulgaria who tossed Slavic children into the air and caught them on the ends of their bayonets, or the one about the Russian parents who smeared their 5-year-old daughter's face and mouth with excrement before locking her for the night in a cold outhouse—was to question how, ultimately, these incidents (and others worse) could ever be justified, even at the end of the age when a divine harmony is to be restored, when all insufferable questions are to be resolved, and when all God's ways are to be forever vindicated before human beings and angels.

"I want to see with my own eyes," thundered Ivan, "the hind lie down with the lion and the victim rise up and embrace his murderer. I want to be there when everyone suddenly understands what it has all been for. . . . But then there are the children, and what am I to do about them? That's a question I can't answer. For the hundredth time I repeat, there are numbers of questions, but I've only taken the children, because in their case what I mean is so unanswerably clear. Listen! If all must suffer to pay for the eternal harmony, what have children to do with it, tell me, please? . . . What good can hell do, since those children have already been tortured? . . . And if the sufferings of children go to swell the sum of sufferings which was necessary to pay for truth, then I protest that the truth is not worth such a price."[2]

Though few can express the words with the grace, the passion, and the fecundity that Dostoyevsky sculpted into Ivan Karamazov's mouth, who hasn't felt that same question grind away at chunks of soul, especially souls who gravitate toward the notion of God? "The children, what am I to do about them?" isn't a query that assaults just the atheist, a conundrum that confronts just the skeptic. (Not that the atheist and the skeptic don't cringe at the children's cries; they do, maybe even more so than theists, because theists can at least hope in some higher, if yet hidden, meaning, whereas for the atheist those cries are nothing but the inevitable noises of a godless, meaningless creation.)

No, "The children, what am I to do about them?" doesn't present the deep philosophical paradoxes to atheists that it does to theists. Children ripped apart by hunting dogs or tortured by parents fit (even nicely) the atheistic weltanschauung; it's the Christian one—with its omnipotent and loving heavenly Father—that appears so inadequately configured to explain even one of these children, much less a whole planet made putrid by them.

"Is God willing to prevent evil, but not able?" asked Epicurus in the third century before Christ. "Then he is not omnipotent. Is he able, but not willing? Then he is malevolent. Is he both able and willing? Then whence cometh evil? Is he neither able nor willing? Then why call him God?"

Many people have, understandably, wondered the same—even those who might find the "moral argument" for the existence of God (as presented in the first chapter) persuasive. If universal moral norms arose only in the human, then any act—from genocide to child pornography—would be moral just as long as people thought it moral. Yet that can't be right, and people know it can't be right, which implies that morality must be rooted in something beyond the human, something transcendent.

For others the approach in the second chapter, which exposes the prevailing a priori materialistic presuppositions of modern secularism and scientism as too narrow, too shallow, and too inadequate to explain humanity, presents evidence for theism. If science can't explain everything (which it can't) and if humanity is more than chemical reactions (which it is)—then perhaps there exists a dimension beyond the stubby, blunt reach of rationality and science alone—a spiritual dimension, a transcendent dimension, a dimension that only God could create.

Then, too, the cosmological argument says that there are only two kinds of possible existence, what's created and what's uncreated. (Try to think of a third.) Now, unless one believes in infinite regress—just one thing created by another with no starting point ever (a position fraught with numerous philosophical difficulties)—how could what's created exist unless it ultimately originated in what's uncreated? How could anything come from nothing? There must be something, therefore, itself uncreated, that didn't originate in anything but had always existed, and what else could that be but God?

For others, the analogical argument, the argument from other minds, gives evidence to justify faith. In the same way that we can know that other minds exist—even though they are invisible, immediately inaccessible to us, and beyond our direct sensory experience—we can, by analogy, believe that God, who is invisible, immediately inaccessible to us, and beyond our direct sensory experience, exists as well. Though not proof of God's existence (it wasn't meant to be), this argument shows that belief in God is at least as justifiable as is belief in other minds.

The teleological argument rationally, even necessarily, arises from the complex design in nature. In whatever direction humanity peers—whether toward the horizon of the cosmos or the nooks and crannies of subatomic particles—the frightful complexity of the simplest things, the flawless fine-tuning of delicate variables, the infinitely subtle symmetry of forces balanced with an unforgiving margin of error, leave almost no option other than a Creator (or at least a Designer).

None of these arguments, in and of itself, proves the existence of God; all of them added together don't either. The arguments are good as far as they go, which isn't far enough; otherwise everyone would believe, which they don't. Instead, these positions show reasonable and logical evidence for faith, nothing more, nothing else.

Yet, however logical or reasonable the evidence, however strong a theistic edifice for faith they form—either alone or woven together in a tapestry of rigorous intellectual consistency—what they don't do, either separately or bunched, is answer or much less even approach Ivan Karamazov's question, "The children, what am I to do about them?"

For many people, those simple one- and two-syllable words of this fictional character have hardened into a solid, immovable wall against which all the logic, all the intellectual rigor, all the reasonableness and rationality of the analogical, the cosmological, the teleological, and all other theistic arguments slam into and are shattered to bloodstained ground in useless and meaningless pieces of linguistic mush, drowned out by the cries of tormented, abused, and diseased children.

Slavic babies bayoneted by Turks as their mothers watched or Dr. Joseph Mengele injecting dye into the eyes of children or removing their organs and limbs without anesthetic are the kinds of events that split open the body and gut the force of these arguments, making them at best irrelevant and at worst problematic for those who believe in the loving God purported to be found at each of their ends.

However logical and reasonable, the proofs are no more logical and reasonable than the question How could the God of the moral, teleological, and cosmological arguments be both all-loving and all-powerful while evil exists? This is, inevitably, the most logical and reasonable question asked in any world on which faith in God coexists with 8-year-old children murdered through the use of hunting dogs.

"If God is perfectly loving," wrote Scottish philosopher John H. Hick, who coined the essential question, "he must wish to abolish evil; and if he is all-powerful, he must be able to abolish evil. But evil exists; therefore God cannot be both omnipotent and perfectly loving."[3]

Unless, however, one understands that omnipotence, by its very nature, comes with inherent limits and that the term itself (as commonly understood) contains an inescapable contradiction. If, with omnipotence, everything were possible—everything!—then that would include the impossible, because "everything," as a universal set, must contain "the impossible" as well. But if God can do everything, impossible things should not be possible; by definition they should be excluded from such a universe. Yet how could they not be possible if omnipotence required the possibility of everything, even "the impossible"? Even with omnipotence, then, the impossible must be possible, which means that omnipotence can't do everything. If He could, impossible things could not exist. This argument isn't sophistry or an exploitation of linguistic contingencies; it simply points out that omnipotence, by its own nature, has limits.

Augustine of Hippo, in the fifth century A.D., examined omnipotence from another angle. "We do not," wrote Augustine in *The City of God* (Book V, chap. 10), "lessen [God's] power when we say He cannot die or be deceived. This is the kind of inability which, if removed, would make God less powerful than He is. God is rightly called omnipotent, even though He is unable to die and be deceived. . . . It is precisely because He is omnipotent that for Him some things are impossible."[4]

Other restraints, inherent not to omnipotence, but to reality itself, bind omnipotence. Can omnipotence create a triangle that has four sides? No, because the moment it has four sides it's no longer a triangle. Can omnipotence create a circle with a square edge? No, because the moment it has a square edge it's no longer a circle. Can omnipotence make $2 + 2 = 5$? No, because the moment it's 5 it's no longer $2 + 2$. And can omnipotence create a love that is forced? No, because the moment that it is forced it's no longer love.

Just as a triangle, to be a triangle, must have three sides, so love, to be love, must be freely given. To force love is to annihilate it. Like a proton meeting an anti-proton, they meet and vanish. Love, by its very definition as love, must be free; otherwise it's not love. Even God, the omnipotent and almighty Creator, cannot create a love that is forced, because the moment it is forced it's something other than love.

Not only, then, does omnipotence contain inherent restraints, but also when coupled with love, those restraints are tightened. God's omnipotence does not mean that He can do all things, and His love means He can do even less. And only in this context, that of the boundaries inhering omnipotence and love, can one begin to understand that it is not a contradiction to argue that God could be omnipotent and loving and yet evil still exist. On the contrary, it would be a contradiction to say that if God were omnipotent and loving, evil could never exist.

Love doesn't necessitate evil. Evil is not an a priori attribute of love, a necessary corollary. What love does necessitate, however, is free choice;

that's an a priori attribute, a necessary corollary. Without freedom, love is as impossible as a Euclidian plane without breadth or width.

God can create obedience without freedom, He can create law without freedom, He can create order without freedom, and He can create compliance without freedom—but not love. God can force the entire universe to worship Him, to obey Him, to fear Him, but He cannot force a single creature in all His creation to love Him.

According to the Gospel of Matthew, however, the first and most important of all commandments is to "love the Lord thy God with all thy heart, and with all thy soul, and with all thy mind" (22:37). How ironic that the first and most important commandment was the only one (unlike adultery, stealing, killing, etc.) that could not be forced, the only one that by its nature has to be freely given or it can't be given at all.

Thus, if it is a prime command, a fundamental human duty, to love God, then a prime and fundamental a priori component of humanity must be freedom—not any kind of freedom but moral freedom, because love is essentially a moral attribute. Only a moral being can love, and only in a moral dimension can love exist. A computer might be programmed to generate a love song, but there's no emotion in the RAM, no passion in the motherboard, no self-denial in the sound card. The existence of love implies a moral dimension in the same way that the existence of matter implies a spatial one. To be able to love God, humans have to be able to make moral choices, and to make those choices, they must have moral freedom. And (here's the crucial pivot, the hinge upon which the question of evil rests) the only way humans can have that moral freedom is if they have the potential to make immoral choices. Without that potential—without the option for immorality or evil—humans are not morally free, and if not morally free, they cannot love.

Moral freedom, of course, doesn't demand that wrong choices be made, only that the potential to make them exists—a crucial distinction (inevitability doesn't inhere to potentiality as potentiality does to inevitability). Without the possibility to do wrong, moral freedom would be an illusion.

Atheist apologist J. L. Mackie has argued that an omnipotent God should have created free beings who would choose to make only good decisions. "If God has made men such," he wrote, "that in their free choices they sometimes prefer what is good and sometimes what is evil, why could he not have made men such that they always freely choose the good? If there is no logical impossibility in a man's freely choosing the good on one, or on several, occasions, there cannot be a logical impossibility in his freely choosing the good on every occasion. God was not, then, faced with a choice between making innocent automata and making beings who, in acting freely, would sometimes go wrong: there was open to him the obviously better possibility of making beings who would act freely but always go right. Clearly, his failure to avail himself of this possibility is inconsistent with his being both omnipotent and wholly good."[5]

Wrong. A person free to make only good choices is free but in the limited sense that a prisoner—if allowed to walk around his cell, use the toilet, or think whatever thoughts he wants—is free. A man locked in a dungeon is, in one sense, free in that his mind isn't chained to a wall. Jean-Paul Sartre argued that a person even under torture is free in whether or not to divulge information. A broader, deeper, and more dimensional freedom, the kind requisite for morality, saps Mackie's argument of vitality because "beings who would act freely but always go right" are arguably neither free nor moral beings.

Though it's not a logical impossibility that free beings would always choose right, to insist that if they don't it is somehow God's fault misses the essential point of what being free entails. God didn't intend to make people who would "sometimes go wrong," as if that were preplanned, as if freedom demanded that they do. Rather, in order to create free people, people capable of moral decisions, God had no choice (again, a situation showing the limits of omnipotence) but to create those who had the potential to do wrong. Otherwise they would not be truly free. The potential must always exist.

"Whether the free men created by God would always do what is right," wrote Alvin Plantinga (in response to Mackie), "would presumably be up to them; for all we know they might sometimes exercise their freedom to do what is wrong."[6]

Morality, to be morality, must possess the potential for immorality, just as love, to be love, must possess the potential not to love. God could have created "men such that they always freely choose the good," but only in a universe where the notions of "freely," "choose," and "the good" are cardboard cutouts of the real.

The argument (essentially) that no free individuals ever created by an omniscient and loving God should ever do immoral acts is simply wrong. Nothing in the notion of an all-loving and omnipotent God demands that the free beings created by Him must always do right. On the contrary, a loving and omnipotent God who creates moral and free beings has, of necessity, to place them in an environment in which evil, though not inevitable, must be possible. The definitions of *moral* and *free* and *loving* demand it. Otherwise, all God could have created were gutless and amoral stick figures. Far from it being a contradiction, then, to say that God is omnipotent, that He is love, and that evil exists, it would be a contradiction to say that because God is omnipotent and is love, therefore evil can never exist.

It does, which is why Ivan's question, "The children, what am I to do about them?" does too. Yet the proof that evil doesn't invalidate either God's love or His omnipotence, far from answering Ivan's question, simply leads to another, even more difficult one. Why did God create free, moral beings capable of love if He knew not only that they had to have the potential for evil but also that they would eventually choose evil?

In order for God to create moral beings, He had to create them free; logic demands that. But why did He have to create those beings to begin with? Freedom is a necessary prerequisite for moral, loving beings, but what prerequisite required that these moral beings be created? Are free moral beings a priori to anything in the universe? What, if anything, has made us a logical necessity in that our nonexistence would entail a fundamental contradiction even for omnipotence?

Nothing, at least nothing apparent. (Some have argued that a loving God needed beings to love Him back, but the giving of love doesn't *require* the receiving of it.) If we are not logically necessary beings, then an omnipotent and all-loving God created us without having had to do so. This must mean, first, that He created us despite His foreknowledge that we would choose evil and, second, that He created us knowing that even if we did choose evil a greater good would arise anyway. If, knowing that the free beings He would create would choose evil, God created those beings anyway, and if God is all-loving, then He must have created those beings with the knowledge that, despite their evil choices, He could ultimately bring about a greater good that reflects His love—no matter how difficult for us (like Ivan Karamazov) to see what that greater good could possibly be.

One of two answers likely exists to Ivan's Karamazov's question.

If the secular, rationalistic view corresponds to reality, then every star in the universe will one day burn out, the era of light will be over, and all life, memory, and consciousness will vanish into the nothingness from which it came. If true, this option means, of course, that Ivan Karamazov's question, "The children, what am I do to about them?" has to be answered somewhat like this: "You can do nothing about the children because all their suffering means nothing. How could it, when one day the stars will burn out, the universe will collapse upon itself, and all matter, space, and time will disappear with absolutely nothing to show for all that came with it, including humanity?"

If, however, the Christian God exists and if His promises are trustworthy, then somehow beyond the stars, somehow beyond the margins of imagination, there's an answer to Ivan's question, and it goes somewhat like this: "There is a greater good, one greater than all that has happened, even to the children, and though that greater good seems impossible even as a possibility, much less a promise—it is a promise, a promise of God."

To believe the first answer means surrendering ourselves and all that we are or could ever be to meaningless, even though deep inside, intimations of meaningfulness tickle our soul—intimations of something transcendent. Otherwise, anything about us that's not beyond us disappears with us. To believe the second position, in contrast, means that hope doesn't need to be chained to gravity, but can lift us to the promise of a greater good beyond even the horizon of the cosmic heat death of the universe.

If, though, one accepts the second answer to Ivan's indomitable question, another even more indomitable one arises. If there is a greater good, if all of God's ways are to be exonerated in a grand and final harmony that vindicates God and all that has happened on earth, how can God justify working it out here in the dirt, in human blood, sweat, and tears, in the children—while He sits enthroned in the glory of heaven?

Whatever the profound questions, whatever the grand moral issues resolved in this struggle between good and evil, however efficiently and permanently the promised answers erase all doubts, iron out all absurdities, and wipe away all tears, the question remains: Why should an omnipotent, omniscient God be safely ensconced somewhere in the sky while, knowing the end from the beginning, He watches us fools crawl on our helpless bellies ignorant of even the next moment, much less the conclusion of all things? Why couldn't whatever point this all-loving God wanted to make be made by Him Himself, rather than with us human beings who are so miserably and inextricably drawn in through no choice of our own?

Good questions all—and only one thing answers them.

The cross.

---

[1] Fyodor Dostoyevsky, *The Brothers Karamazov,* pp. 272, 273.

[2] *Ibid.,* pp. 274, 275.

[3] John Hick, quoted in *Philosophy: An Introduction Through Literature,* ed. Lowell Kleiman and Stephen Lewis (New York: Paragon House, 1992), p. 457.

[4] Augustine, *The City of God,* trans. Gerald G. Walsh et al. (New York: Doubleday, 1958), p. 109.

[5] J. L. Mackie, "Evil and Omnipotence," *Mind* 64 (1955): 209.

[6] Alvin Plantinga, *God and Other Minds* (Ithaca, N.Y.: Cornell University Press, 1967), p. 139.

[Chapter 5]

Other People's Pain

In the final analysis," wrote Nietzsche, "one experiences only oneself."[1]

Nietzsche is right. When we grieve with the grieving, weep with the weeping, and suffer with the suffering, we experience only our own grief, only our own cries, and only our own anguish—never anyone else's. We bleed our own blood, spew our own spit, secrete our own sweat—never another's, no matter how fused our flesh. Other people's pain comes to us filtered, always and only, through our own; our own, then, is all we ever know.

"What were you doing," wrote Annie Dillard, "on April 30, 1991, when a series of waves drowned 138,000 people? Where were you when you first heard the astounding, heartbreaking news? Who told you? What, seriatim, were your sensations? Who did you tell? Did you weep? Did your anguish last days or weeks?"[2]

However much you cried, however loud your anguish, it was still only your own cries, only your own anguish (no one else's), just as each of those 138,000 drowning persons felt only their own lungs—and no one else's—clog with the cold, choking water. Whether a mother holding a feverish infant to her breast or a husband clutching a crumpled wife, neither can splice into the nerves of the other in order to feel a spasm of their woe, a prick of their pain, or a sputter of their sorrow. No matter how loud, outrageous, or consuming, pain remains more private than thought itself. Thought can always be shared; pain never can. Unlike the liver, the heart, or blood, suffering is nontransferable and nontransplantable. What's yours is yours alone.

When famine descended upon Ethiopia and tons of flesh withered and faded back into the earth, they did so one quivering ounce at a time. However we die, however we suffer—whether alone or in bundles—corporate agony, collective pain, doesn't exist; we are islands of anguish unto ourselves.

This privatization of pain, this personalization of anguish, is good—because it means that no one has ever suffered more than an individual can. Grief remains finite, hedged in always by what's as minuscule and as evanescent as the human. We know no more suffering than our personal metabolism allows, no more pain than our delirious cells can carry. No matter how many miles of nerves are wired through us, what are they but a few frayed and twisted threads in contrast to the light-years of reality that engulf us? Our finitude is our defense, our physical boundaries our best protection. How fortunate that pain and suffering remain hedged in and limited by the inherent confines of individuality. It's hard enough, this bearing of our own pain; imagine carrying others' as well!

There's an exception, however, to this otherwise pandemic personalization of pain—only one time when this universal paradigm of individuated anguish shifted. And though, after this seminal event, a line joining a planet in orbit around the sun still swept out equal areas in equal intervals of time, and Planck's constant was still 6.626×10^{-34} joule-seconds and objects at rest still stayed at rest until acted upon by an outside force, after this event—Christ dying on the cross—the moral center of the universe radically and irreversibly changed.

This is the cross now. Not religion, not dogma, not creeds, not traditions, not doctrines, not councils, not churches, and not Christians (especially not Christians). This is the cross, and the cross alone, undiluted and uncorrupted by churches, decrees, councils, traditions, and Christians that so distorted the view that for millions the only cross they know dangles from Madonna's neck.

If one could shovel away the debris, climb over the rubble, and wade past the moral and physical wreckage left in the wake of 2,000 years of Christian history in order to see the cross, what would appear? If uncorrupted by politics, undistorted by tradition, and unencumbered by dogmas, what would the cross be? If one could peel off the cross centuries of ecclesiastical scum, what would remain? If one could unravel all presuppositions and epistemic prejudices amassed from lifetimes of lies, myths, and religious illusions—all in order to have a clear, unadulterated, and undistorted view of the cross—what's there?

They would see a contrast that language is too flimsy, too flaccid, and too parochial to reflect, a mystery that the mind isn't wired deeply and profoundly enough to contain without spilling mostly over the sides. Language barely approaches it, words rudely sketch it, poetry bludgeons it. Our minds aren't refined enough to reproduce it, because the serotonin is too diluted, the synapses too blunt. All that appears is outline, yet even that's overwhelming.

What they would see at the cross is the Creator of the universe: the Being who spoke the strong force, the weak force, electromagnetism, and gravity into existence, the Being who sprinkled infinity with the Eagle Nebula and Orion, the Being who threaded 100 billion billion superstring loops into every proton, the One upon whom all that exists rests—shrunk into human flesh and nailed to two pieces of wood, His life crushed out by all the pain, suffering, and anguish of a world that, in His preexistent state, He with His own creative syllables had crafted into existence.

Though we experience only our own fear, only our own loathing, no one else's—at the cross, Jesus experienced everyone else's. The individual miseries of humanity were one by one added up, and the gruesome sum fell on Him. At the cross everything noisome and evil that ever rippled through our nerves rippled through His—at once.

Here, and here alone, the questions asked earlier find answers. If there is a greater good, if all of God's ways are to be exonerated in a grand and final harmony that vindicates Him and all that has happened on earth, how can He justify working it out here, in the dirt, in human blood, sweat, and tears, in the children—while He sits enthroned in the glory of heaven?

Whatever the profound questions, whatever the grand moral issues resolved in this struggle between good and evil, however efficiently and permanently the promised answers erase all doubts and iron out all absurdities, and wipe away all tears, the question remains: Why should an omnipotent, omniscient God be safely ensconced somewhere while, knowing the end from the beginning, He watches us fools crawl on our helpless bellies, ignorant of even the next moment, much less the conclusion of all things?

Why couldn't whatever point this all-loving God wants to make be made by Him Himself, rather than with us human beings who are so miserably and inextricably drawn in through no choice of our own?

These questions are fiercely, unequivocally, and forever answered. However much blood, sweat, and tears have dripped under anemic moons, despite the cancerous color of the soul and the loathsome fates of little ones—none of them, none of us, has suffered more than a single human can. Our pain has never surpassed our finitude. No one has ever ached more than he or she, individually, could withstand. The moment the threshold was crossed, death put an end to it.

In contrast, far from God's remaining safely ensconced somewhere in the sky, at the cross the evils of the world and all their doleful results homed in on Him. From the children mutilated and then murdered by Mengele to even the Herr Doktor's personal tremors of guilt, from the first swollen belly to the last tarred lung, from abused to abuser, all the planet's finite evils fell on the infinite God incarnated in Jesus Christ, and, amassed at once, they were enough to kill even Him.

Putting aside postmodern mumbling about relativism, pluralism, perspectivism, about Foucault's interpretative analysis or Derrida's deconstruction of the text or Wittgenstein's language games . . . either England is an island in Europe or it isn't; either Jonathan Swift wrote *A Tale of a Tub* or he didn't; either George Washington was the prime minister of France from 1926 to 1937 or he wasn't; and either at the cross the Creator of the universe, having taken upon Himself humanity, died from the evil of that humanity or He didn't.

There's no middle ground here, no compromise. Either Jesus Christ was God Himself incarnate, or He was just a good man (and there exists an infinite qualitative difference between the two), or maybe He was even a bad man, or maybe never a man at all. But if He were merely a good man, or a great one, or even the greatest—yet not God, too—then the cross would be as noxious a lie as it is as wonderful a truth. (The insidiousness of the fraud is proportional to the greatness of the fact.)

If God is merely an invention of man, then man invented not only God but also One who suffered infinitely more than the creature, any creature, He created. Belief in a false god is bad enough; belief in a crucified one is even worse, for while the belief helps tame the cruel, empty spaces of the universe, the lie makes them more hellish than ever.

However incredible the cross, nothing is contradictory there. To affirm it doesn't automatically deny it. The Power who uttered into existence infinity, eternity, and matter, wrapping them together and draping the result across nothing, certainly would have the potential to garb Himself in human flesh and then die in that flesh. The One who created all of what's created could become part of what's created. The issue is not physics (How did He do it?) but morality (Why did He?).

If ascending from zero to one takes an infinite step, what's the moral calculus of descending from the infinite to the finite? That God Himself would become a human being, that the infinite would assume finitude (while still remaining infinite), that's incredible enough. But that God would, in the form of finitude, suffer only as the infinite could suffer? Logic and reason knuckle under the notion. Before a sketch, even a rough draft, the imagination surrenders. Only the metaphysics of faith can approach it.

If it's true that the Creator Himself took on the form of humanity and died in behalf of humanity a death not only worse than the worst of the best of humanity but a death worse than all of humanity (even the worst of it) combined, then the moral geometry of reality has to be reconsidered. The proportions, lines, postulates, emphases, foci, and angles have to be exhumed, reexamined, and, if need be (how could they not be?), re-done—something more radical than the shift from Euclidean to Riemannian geometry. If true, the hues, the tones, the tenor of the cosmos change—and the music of the spheres becomes howling praise.

Even if you don't believe, think (for a gilded moment) what it would mean if you did. Suppose you could step outside the epistemological box stapled together from the empirical, cultural, and happenstance scraps scavenged from your own intellectual turf only to discover that the most important thing you can ever know is something that you could never deduce or induct, but instead—being too solid, too objective for reason and empiricism alone (which only paw at it)—it has to be told you, no, spoon-fed to you in revelatory drips and dribbles?

Suppose you could peel away the opaque curtain of the phenomenon and get to the noumenon, only to discover that it was made by a God who had become human and died a death worse than all that's human combined, a death that has bound us to Him with bonds tighter than that which holds together space and time. This would mean that we, us, our sufferings, rather than dissipating into meaninglessness, are woven into the essence of creation.

Suppose you believed that the ultimate reality, in which all else can be resolved and that cannot itself be resolved into anything else wasn't something physical but rather was moral, wasn't superstring loops but a love that stretches across the cold expanses of infinity into the feverish recesses of our fearful, expiring lives? And suppose that you believed that the incarnate God Himself, out of love for each of us, hung on the cross for all of us as the only way to give any of us something more than the option of (1) getting sick and dying old, (2) getting sick and dying young, or (3) just dying young. Also, suppose that's the promise of a new and imperishable existence in which none of the above are options.

If God in Jesus Christ "tasted death for all men" (see Hebrews 2:9), if He died "for the sins of the whole world" (1 John 2:2), and if upon Him was placed the iniquity "of us all" (Isaiah 53:6)—then all of us are implicated in the cross, because all of our evil was there.

Again, either the cross is true or it's a lie.

If a lie, then it's just another murdered Jew, a black hole into which much hope, promise, and prayer have been poured, with little or nothing in return.

But, if it's true, then your lies, your greed, your envy, your lust, your pride, your cheating, your selfishness—all the nasty and dirty little things you have thought and done, things that by themselves might not seem so bad but if added up, shoved in your face, and exposed for what they really were would cause you to claw at your own flesh—were there at the cross. So when all the evil moments of your life are tallied and weighed, they don't have to kill you ultimately and forever.

There's no justice in this life. But if God exists and if He is just, then justice will be done. This means that sooner or later you'll have to answer for everything, for the dirty secrets that occasionally appear in drag in your dreams, for the pangs that itch in places where you can't scratch, and even for all the things that you long ago justified with the coldness of quadratic equations and then conveniently forgot. Imagine facing every evil thought, word, and deed at once, with all excuses, rationalizations, and justifications swept away by the peering eye of an all-seeing, all-knowing God who exposes the deepest, most carnal motives until there's nowhere to hide before the One whom even the clearest conscience is opaque with evil.

If all the evil you have ever committed or ever will commit fell on Jesus in order to spare you from the punishment that justice demands, then the cross has an absolute moral claim on you. Whether you believe it or not, whether you accept it or not, the claim remains, and all other ties, in contrast, bind you in nothing but pink ribbons and bows. No one, nothing else, has such a stake in you because no one, nothing else, has done (or could do) so much for you.

If at the cross Christ paid the penalty for every wrong thing you have ever done, if He bore the brunt of your evil, if in His flesh He felt at once the painful consequences of your foul deeds, and if He did it in order to spare you from having to face divine retribution for all these things you have done, and you reject the provision—then what?

That's heavy. Whatever we do or have done to others we do or have done to those of our own noisome brew, those who are mere fun house reflections of ourselves. We are finite creatures who do things—sometimes petty, sometimes puerile, sometimes terrible, but always and only finite and temporal things, nothing more. The gap between who we are, what we do, and to whom we do them stays finite, and the finite minus the finite equals finitude.

The cross, however, presents to humanity something infinite, something eternal. Instead of hovering "out there" as concepts merely sensed or intuited, that which is infinite and eternal stepped directly into the equations of our lives, wrote Himself into the formulas of our immediate existence, and made Himself accessible as never before. To have the eternal and infinite God clothe Himself in temporal flesh in order to save us from the inevitable doom of our own rotting wraps . . . only to have those temporal and rotting wraps purposely reject what He did for us?

There's an infinite gap between the finite and the infinite. Those who have rejected what Jesus has done for them have, in a sense, breached that gap; it is the ultimate transgression because it is an infinite one. Of all the evil of the world at the cross—the murders, the rapes, the incest, the barbarity—the only one not there, the only one not provided for, is the only one that's infinite, the one in which the finite rejects the Infinite. (Infinity minus finitude equals infinity.)

But what about those who have never heard of the cross or never had it presented accurately to them? Are they, by default, doomed?

It could hardly seem so. First, who can blatantly reject what they've never known? Second, if at the cross the evil of the world fell on the incarnate God, that includes all evil, even that of those who have never heard of Jesus. Why would Jesus Christ bear that loathsome load if these people weren't somehow offered the option of eternity, however much the particulars might have dangled before them distorted, disguised, or even denied by their own tribal deities? Jesus Christ as God incarnate didn't go through the anguish of the cross for them or for anyone else, carte blanche, for nothing.

Besides, the immediate issue isn't those who never heard of the cross. The issue, instead, is those who have heard, those who have been given an image of the Infinite squeezed into finite flesh and then crushed by the world's evil. Only two logical responses exist. The first is to dismiss the image outright as a hellish myth; a nasty, fatal kink in the DNA. The second is to fall before it broken, amazed, and transformed because of the wonderful hope offered through such incomprehensible grace.

Yet the second option, that of belief, isn't tautological with loving and lovable Christians. On the contrary. Corporate Christianity has tended to produce corporate wretches. It's one thing to have vile folks walk into a church (that's to be expected); it is another matter to have them leave worse because their villainy is now absolved by a conscience confirmed in the certainty of terminal truth.

How does one explain those who have murdered, raped, and pillaged in the name of Jesus? What about those God-fearing churchgoing Protestants in the American South who loved the Lord Jesus but wouldn't share their toilets with a Black person? Or what about the folks who shoved Jews into gas chambers on Monday through Saturday but rested from their works on Sunday?

From the Crusades to the Inquisition, from the Ku Klux Klan to the most orthodox Fascists, why has Christianity provided the vehicle, the incentive, and the rationale for so much of what rots the planet? And why has much of what's been noxious been nurtured in the cold, lurid womb of the church, which served for centuries as the intellectual, cultural, and moral dungeon of the West?

Though good questions, none are good excuses. Jesus Himself warned about those who would, under the guise of Christian faith, work iniquity: "Not every one that saith unto me, Lord, Lord, shall enter into the kingdom of heaven; but he that doeth the will of my Father which is in heaven. Many will say to me in that day, Lord, Lord, have we not prophesied in thy name? and in thy name have cast out devils? and in thy name done many wonderful works? And then will I profess unto them, I never knew you: depart from me, ye that work iniquity" (Matthew 7:21-23).

Millions of professed Christians have, for almost 2,000 years, provided convenient excuses to reject the cross. What they haven't provided are adequate ones, because nothing has changed the cross, where God in human flesh died for and from the world's evil—an infinite act that transcends all finite ones, even the ones done in the name of the act itself. Nothing nullifies the cross. It remains above and beyond all else, and its claims are so universal, so sweeping, and so grand that they blow away all excuses, even the good ones. They have to go.

The issue isn't Christians, or churches, or councils, or creeds. The issue, instead and only, is the cross, the pivot point upon which human destiny hinges, the place where reality divided into two eternal options.

With such high stakes, with the results so consequential, with the intensity of what God incarnate went through for every human, it hardly makes sense for Him to do anything other than give those who have heard reasons to believe. Why go through all that He did—which does no one who doesn't believe any ultimate good—without providing enough evidence to believe?

He didn't, and we do.

---

[1] Friedrich Nietzsche, *Thus Spoke Zarathustra,* trans. R. J. Hollingdale (New York: Penguin Books, 1969), p. 173.

[2] Annie Dillard, "The Wreck of Time," *Harper's,* January 1998, p. 53.

[Chapter 6]

The Child, Unmodified

We don't see things as they are," says the Talmud. "We see them as we are."

If true, then reality comes to us at a slant. And the truer the thought, the steeper the slant, until the world confronts us all upside down (which is why our brain turns it right side up). That which is outside of us appears to us according to that which is *inside* us, and that which is within us varies not only from person to person but also within each person. Thus, existence is partitioned into nothing but consciousness (that is, *individual* consciousness) modified by everything from grandfather's temper and serotonin metabolism to the sugar content of breakfast.

"The world," said Arthur Schopenhauer, "is my idea."[1]

If it's Arthur's idea, then it's yours. And if yours, then it's your bitterest foe's, too. What man knows (said Schopenhauer) is "not a sun, and not an earth, but only an eye that sees a sun, a hand that feels an earth; that the world which surrounds him exists only as idea—that is, only in relation to something else, the one who conceives the idea, which is himself."[2]

And because we are different eyes, different hands, different consciousnesses, we know different suns and different earths. (Was it Ra in his chariot that sailed into Galileo's telescope with such harsh light? Was it Gaia who seduced the coal miner's lung?) If the world is (at least for us) idea, then the world is a different idea for each of us, and because ideas clash, we do too.

Imago dei or a cannibal's lunch? A dangerous felon or a favorite son? An act of God or plate tectonics? Terrorism or national liberation? When one's axioms are another's lies; when one's postulates are another's parody; when the cosmogonic, deontological, and teleological truths of a nation are mocked as tales, superstitions, and myths by the *demos* of their neighbors;

when one's God sports horns and a tail in the consciousness of another; when a face that adorns placards and statutes is, across an artificial border, pasted on wanted posters—clash is inevitable. Conflicts occur, then, not so much over what *is* but over what's *thought to be.*

This question about what's real as opposed to what's perceived stretches back at least to Plato's cave. "Imagine," Plato wrote, "an underground chamber like a cave, with a long entrance open to the daylight and as wide as the cave. In this chamber are men who have been prisoners here since they were children, their legs and necks being so fastened that they can only look straight ahead of them and cannot turn their heads. Some way off, behind and higher up, a fire is burning, and between the fire and the prisoners and above them runs a road, in front of which a curtain-wall has been built, like the screen at puppet shows between the operators and their audience, above which they show their puppets. . . . For, tell me, do you think our prisoners could see anything of themselves or their fellows except the shadows thrown by the fire on the wall of the cave opposite of them? . . . Then, if they were able to talk with each other, would they not assume that the shadows they saw were the real things?"[3]

Only through philosophical and rational education, argued Plato, could anyone escape the cave and ascend into the world of sunlight—reality as it truly is contrasted to the default mode of penumbras, shadows, and shades that now clog our senses. However apt (or crude) Plato's metaphor, what would there be if we could slip out, climb over, and get behind appearances, sensations, and phenomena in order to explore reality as it is *in itself* without the innate human filters that color, categorize, and package it for us as appearances, sensations, and phenomena? What does the elusive *ding an sich* look like, feel like, smell like, taste like? All we know of reality, even that which arises from pure reason alone, comes to us only as neuro-electrical-chemical processes that ignite quietly within a soggy darkness covered by skin, skull, and meninges.

Suppose, however, that quanta of Kool-aid brand soft drink instead of serotonin swooped across these wet clefts. What new worlds would appear in our consciousness? Suppose our neurons were twice as big or twice as small, twice as long or twice as short, twice as thick or twice as thin as those that wire us now. What reality would project itself into our souls?

Suppose that up quarks were down and down quarks were up or that a formula in the physics of the brain differed by .0005^{-67} percent; what different axioms would Peano have discovered, what new laws of motion would have been wrenched out of the air, and what would the new age of consent be?

If no eye could ever detect the narrow bands of electromagnetic waves that translate to red and blue in our heads, what would be the colors of arid noon or a muffled sunset? (We know only what two colors they could *never* be.) What if our ears could detect the fear in birds, our noses the floating codes of flowers, our fingers the wind of electrons?

Reality would appear different, for sure, but would a rewired mind attached to more acute sensors give us a better picture, or one just as subjective as the 3-D show now running between our ears?

Even if it were possible to slip out, climb over, and get behind appearances, sensations, and phenomena to perceive reality, how could we perceive it with anything but other senses? But senses *of any kind* always have biases in their wires, limits in their tissues, and preconceptions in their receptors. Whatever sensors connect us to what's outside us; whatever devices interface us with the world; whatever peripherals funnel images, sounds, tastes, and smells into our minds—each has its own focus, slant, and boundaries. Different combinations create different realities. (How many millions have been murdered because of a single degree of deviation in the cephalic index?) How, then, can reality be anything more than the subjective, limited senses perceiving it—which means, then, that reality would have to be all in our heads, nowhere else.

Might it be that only if there were a being—some divine Mind—who could view all things from every possible perspective, every possible angle, and every possible position at the same time that objective reality could even be said to exist? Can, as Bishop George Berkeley argued, something really be anything, that is, have innate characteristics or qualities not ultimately in a mind perceiving them (because what ultimately are characteristics or qualities [hot, cold, red, yellow, sweet, sour, hard, soft] other than sense impressions)? And how can sense impressions exist without a mind to sense them? How can there be pain without nerves, or taste without sensors? And because different minds (as well as different nerves and sensors) perceive the same things differently, without some ultimate omniscient Mind that knows and perceives everything from every possible perspective, angle, and position, can there ever be any reality other than what's subjectively experienced by different minds? Without a divine Mind, does it make sense even to talk about what's *truly* out there? Otherwise, that which is out there is only subjective, fluctuating, and often time-deceptive sense impressions, nothing more.

Two people, one used to spicy food and one not, eat chili peppers. One says that they're hot; the other that they're not. Are chili peppers—in reality (as opposed to mere personal taste)—hot or not? Can it be one or the other (or even anything) independent of a mind perceiving it as one or the other or as something else entirely?

These questions are the ontological parallel to the deontological one posed in the chapter "Trinkets of Death." Can there be true morality (or true reality) if all morality (or reality) exists only as electrical and chemical reactions in subjective, vacillating minds? We intuit that morality exists independent of us. Otherwise, how can murdering babies only because they're Jewish be immoral if every human mind thinks otherwise? We intuit, even more so, that reality exists independent of minds. Otherwise, is Mount Everest nonexistent if no mind perceives it? But how can moral and ontological absolutes exist if both morality and existence are found only in minds, not outside them?

The implications of these questions have been debated for centuries. British empiricist John Locke argued that if human knowledge arises from only experience, then how can we know anything of itself? Knowledge can go no further than experience. Nothing exists in the intellect, he wrote, that was not first in the senses. And because that which is in the senses is always limited, contingent, and in flux (a dark room, after a few minutes, often doesn't seem as dark), we're left with little real knowledge of the world.

Pushing his own empiricist presuppositions further, Bishop George Berkeley articulated his famous formula, *esse est percipi* ("To be is to be perceived"), claiming that qualities and characteristics of things, even their most primary qualities (such as extension) don't have existence outside of the mind. He argued that only as an object is perceived can it be said to exist. "For what are the forementioned objects [houses, mountains, rivers] but things we perceive by sense?" he wrote. "And what do we perceive *besides our own ideas or sensations?* and is it not plainly repugnant that any one of these, or any combination of them, should exist unperceived?"[4]

Because reality appears only as sensation, there's no sensation (hence, no reality) that's unperceived. Bishop Berkeley was not denying that these things are there. Instead, he was saying that when something is said "to exist," it means only that it is perceived by a mind. For how can the phrase "to exist"—that is, to have qualities (and what are qualities except things perceived in minds [hot, cold, red, large, spicy]?)—ever be used to describe anything without the assumption of mind there to perceive them?

"For only after men," wrote Schopenhauer, "had tried their hand for thousands of years at a mere philosophy of the object did they discover that, among the many things that make the world so puzzling and give us pause for thought, is first and foremost that, however immeasurable and massive this world may be, its existence hangs nonetheless by a single thread: that is, the actual consciousness in which it exists."[5]

Assuming the reality of a priori synthetic propositions, upon which he based his revolutionary philosophy, Prussian philosopher Immanuel Kant argued that the mind itself construes reality. Not that it *creates* reality (in the sense of, for instance, putting a Lexus four-wheel drive where otherwise there was only a Volkswagen Beetle), but that as a result of preexisting structures within them, our minds synthesize and unify reality not according to the world itself but according to the mind itself. The mind, as it were, imposes itself upon the world, which appears only as it is organized, filtered, and categorized by mind. Mind doesn't conform to the world; the world conforms to the mind. Our brains don't change the world-as-it-is (Kant wrote long before the quantum revolution); the world as-it-is comes to us only as our brain allows. We see not what's really "out there" but only skewed slices according to what our brains, through preexisting categories and structures, present to us. The brain, in essence, functions as an a priori censor of all reality.

A person looking at a mountain through binoculars will see something different than a person looking at it through a microscope. The mountain is there, for sure, but what we see depends on whether our mind works like a microscope or like binoculars or like a pair of human eyes that catch only a notch of electromagnetic waves and that bend those waves (according to the bulges and sags of the cornea) in a certain way. After the eyes refract these light rays, the results are processed along predetermined electrochemical neurological clefts that in a specific, highly refined manner project the ideas and sensations of human consciousness. (Different notches, sags, and clefts create different ideas, sensations, and consciousness.)

Unlike the latter phenomenalistic idealists (such as Johann Gottlieb Fichte), who would do away with all reality other than that which exists in our minds (after all, why bother with what you can never know?), Kant didn't reject the noumenon, that is, reality independent of human cognition. The phenomenon (how reality appears to us) can't exist without noumena (how reality really is) any more than pain can exist without nerves. What Kant asserts, instead, is that we can never *know* noumena, the real world. An impenetrable, dark divide hangs between what's there and how—after having run the gauntlet of the mind (where after being quantified, qualified, bowdlerized, homogenized, and whatever else), it finally appears as reality in our consciousness.

None of these philosophers, of course, and none of their philosophies, have remained uncontested. Nevertheless, it's hard to argue against the basic point: the limits of knowledge, especially knowledge that comes through sensory perception alone. Writing against the Protagoran maxim that "man is the measure of all things," Plato said that if all that were requisite for truth were sensation, then a "pig or a dog-faced baboon" would also be the "measure of all things."

Plato's point is that reality can't be measured and judged by human standards only, because different individuals measure and judge reality differently, even contradictorily. The argument that there's no objective reality apart from the senses—though defensible with some logical and rational rigor (which, as with quantum theory, reveals the limits of logic and rational rigor)—remains if nothing else intuitively unconvincing, particularly to someone who barely survived going headfirst through a windshield. He knows that something real, solid, objective in-and-of-itself exists outside of himself, whatever the epistemic limits inherent in explaining what that reality in-and-of-itself is.

Kant's division between noumenon and phenomenon has been validated in the twentieth century in ways unimaginable to eighteenth-century Immanuel. How many cell phone calls, radio waves, and satellite images engulf us? What spasms of sex, what acoustical triptychs, what twitters and twangs gurgle silently in the electronic matrix around our ears? How much twisted syntax streams through wafts of lunch and pulses behind the unruly rhythms squeezed through our window frames?

Yet given our specific wiring and the limited peripherals plugged into them, the spasms, the twitters, and the twangs—unlike the wakes of French fries and the cry of bus brakes—don't tweak our noses or twiddle our ears. We're stranded on the short end of Immanuel Kant's gap, the cold dark divide between noumenon and phenomenon—a gap no mortal has yet crossed. What could a mortal view the noumena with other than more or different or even better sensory devices that merely project other limited images into biased neurons that always process them with an a priori prejudice?

Only a divine Mind—one knowing all things conceivable and inconceivable, one taking in everything potential and realized—has access to the *ding an sich*. The rest of us are left with empirical detritus only, the musty shades and watery umbra of mind.

From Plato's cave to Kant's epistemological cant, the question remains: What else is out there, what else moves, exists, lives across the gap between the narrow, finite spectrum of appearances in human minds and the wide, infinite spectrum of the real? (After all, is not reality infinite?) Like high-pitched sounds that only dog's ears catch or like subatomic particles from space that enter our heads and come out the bottom of our feet (sounds and particles just as real as soccer balls and Bach cantatas), what else exist as noumena that we just can't sense, see, feel, or intuit?

Scientists talk of other dimensions beyond space-time. A few branches of physics demand them. (Superstring theory calls for at least 10.) Some mathematicians argue that pure numbers themselves exist in an independent "reality" distinct from our world of sense perception. Others have argued that the supernatural, the occult, the realm of faith and angels and the preternatural, the realm of raw good and evil apart from the contingencies and limitations of humanity, exists in the noumenon.

The author of the New Testament book of Hebrews wrote that the "things which are seen were not made of things which do appear" (Hebrews 11:3). The apostle Paul talked about realities "that are in heaven, and that are in earth, visible and invisible" (Colossians 1:16). What are those things that do not appear? What are those invisible realities, if not so much in heaven but on earth?

Kant's distinction between the phenomenon and the noumenon,

though not proving the presence of the supernatural (certainly this was not his intention), has at least provided a room for it at the inn. He forged, if nothing else, a feasible metaphysical abode—a place where, were the supernatural to exist, it could exist. A million cell phone calls buzzing about us imply the *possibility*—not the *probability* or even the *plausibility*—of other intangibles too. (Angels, maybe?) The first shows, if nothing else, that intelligent, purposeful activity can function all around us yet remain beyond us even when it impacts us. Who, for instance, smelled, heard, saw, tasted, or touched the high levels of radiation that destroyed their intestinal lining, weakened their immune system, and killed them?

Noumenon matters in more ways than one, and all the time, too. Phenomenon is, perhaps, nothing but the corner of noumenon that mind rubs against and absorbs, like a soggy dark sponge. That we don't touch all of it doesn't mean that we don't touch some. That we can't know it fully doesn't mean that we can't know it partially. In Exodus, when Moses asked God, "Show me your glory" (Exodus 33:18, NIV), God replied, "You cannot see my face, for no one may see me and live." And the Lord said, "There is a place near me where you may stand on a rock. When my glory passes by, I will put you in a cleft in the rock and cover you with my hand until I have passed by. Then I will remove my hand and you will see my back; but my face must not be seen" (verses 20-23, NIV). Maybe that's all the phenomenon is, the back and not the face, of the noumenon.

Mathematicians have encountered incredible coherence and beauty in the world of numbers. Mathematics seems to be "out there" (as the West Indies were for Columbus), not as physical structures, but rather as precise and delicate relations between nonextended, preexisting entities more permanent and firm than is the material world. However highly processed by the brain, something's still there, something these mathematicians encounter as realities that appear more consistent, reliable, and stable than the fleeting, vacillating, and ersatz vagaries of phenomenon. Three kilos of French Blend from Starbucks, no matter how accurate the scale, will always be more or less than three kilos (even if off by a few molecules). However, the number 3, as a number alone, is absolute, refined, and pure. It has no need of any, even the most subtle or delicate, refining.

Thus, whether as concept or sensation, something of the noumenon does get through, even if it feels only like phenomenon. (How else could it feel?) We're made, as it were, to interact with noumenon or at least part of it. There's a comfortable harmony, a convenient and even aesthetically pleasing concord, between our senses and the portion of reality (the "back") that enters our consciousness.

How fortunate that we can view the part of the electromagnetic spectrum cast by the star closest to our eyes in a way that not only allows us to see objects but also to see them so beautifully. Is there any logical, necessary, or even practical reason for sunsets or peacocks to be portrayed so pleasantly in our minds? Whatever the *ding an sich* that rises from mint, how nice that by the time it goes through the nose it is a sensuous fragrance in the mind. Sexual pleasure, as phenomenon alone, is wonderful enough. (As noumenon it would kill us all!) Whatever an orange (or a peach or a plum or a grape) is in-and-of-itself, it not only lusciously and tastefully interacts with our mouths but also comes saturated with chemicals and nutrients that just happen to harmonize with our physical needs. (How gratifying too, given the aesthetic contours of our mouths, that oranges—not acorns or pinecones—are filled with vitamin C!)

Natural selection purports to explain why we need to see the tiger, but not why its stripes arrive inside our minds with such raw grace and elegance. (Besides, wouldn't the fittest *Homo sapiens* better survive if these dangerous beasts were ugly, fearsome-faced, and unattractive?)

The anthropic principle (from the Greek word *anthropos,* man) says that only in a universe capable of sustaining human life could humans even be there to see it, but it doesn't say why so much appears lovely to the human minds that see it. After all, the same alpine sunset that makes us ogle-eyed probably (given the a priori structures of its mind) does nothing for a frog. However great the distance between the noumenon and what's perceived, that which we perceive is often packaged so pleasantly and sensuously that our sensors seem made for the distinct purpose of funneling noumenon to us in intensely satisfying ways.

Of course, the same devices that project good and pleasure into our consciousness do the same with evil and ugliness. The sunset that drains incandescent puddles of light from the horizon also leaves behind a cold wake for those crouched and quivering in unfriendly doorways. And whatever its anarchic wonders, sexual ecstasy often comes with suppurating sores, colonies of bacteria, and unwanted conceptions that bounce genetic anguish across generations. However luscious a grape or tasty an apple, famine and pestilence often break them down before the human belly does. And that belly—the whole human body even (anatomical and physiological marvels all)—also provides lush fodder and rich feed for a pastiche of rapacious tumors. Thus, however inherently good the phenomenon, evil often soils the package.

Evil, however, is *after* the fact. And the fact itself—as pure fact—*is good*. Augustine, in *The City of God,* wrote that evil is a diminishment, a defection, of the good. The good came first. Evil followed, an apostasy from the postulate, a paralogism from the axiom. There is no efficient cause of evil, said Augustine, only a deficient one. "What we call evil," he wrote, "is merely a lack of something that is good."[6]

Like silence and darkness, evil arises only from a lack, from a falling away. According to Augustine, "trying to discover causes of such defections—causes which, as I have said, are not efficient but deficient—is like trying to see darkness or hear silence. True, we have some knowledge of both darkness and silence: of the former only by the eyes; of the latter only by the ears. Nevertheless, we have no sensation but only the privation of sensation."[7]

Look closely. A rotted peach demands, first, the peach. (In reality, not in grammar, the noun must precede the adjective.) There can be no sexual disease without, first, sex. And behind the abused child exists only the child. Like cracks in the pietà or the blotch on a banana, these adjectives are secondary and unoriginal intrusions that are *after* the fact. But the fact itself, as pure fact, is good.

Children, peaches, sex—before any deficiency, antecedent to any defect—reveal the creative touch of a tender, genteel love. Think of them, edited of all unintended adjectives; imagine the child, unmodified.

But even now it's there, in the subtle curves of the peach, in the deep echoes of sex, and all through the child. It's dripping off the trees even, more apparent than air, and we sense it even if we're afraid to say it for fear of sounding silly or unscientific. However rudely deflowered, nature still can transcend parched logic and sprinkle us with hints of something more hopeful than cosmic entropy. Between what's in us (our senses) and what's out there (the sensed), the equations beautifully compute, the numbers work majestically, even if they have to be tallied in our hearts, not in our heads, because in that soggy darkness of the mind so many bad adjectives and adverbs have been soaked up that it's too polluted to get past its own modifiers, much less those that have clawed their way into prime facts.

The previous chapter, "Other People's Pain," posited the almost incredible claim that God Himself had become incarnated into humanity, that the Creator of the universe had assumed our flesh and at the cross and in that flesh bore every evil adjective and adverb (and every evil verb and noun). And the weight of all that perfidy—its guilt, its consequence, its penalty—was enough to kill Him. God isn't immune to our pain and evil. On the contrary, they crushed out His life, as manifested in Jesus on the cross.

But if the cross is true, it's true only because God loves us with a love (as the previous chapter said) that stretched "across the cold expanses of infinity into the feverish recesses of our fearful, expiring lives." It said, too, that with issues so consequential, so terminal, God incarnate wouldn't have gone to the cross without giving us reasons to believe that He did, and this chapter asserts that one of those reasons exists in the unmodified facts themselves. Imagine creation stripped of all its foul modifiers, and then imagine those modifiers falling, at once, upon Jesus.

Creation doesn't *prove* that God made us or died for us. It can't. It proves only that the hypothesis of God, of a *loving* God, isn't empirically implausible. The logic behind the notion doesn't require irrational or imaginary numbers—positive whole numbers will do. Faith doesn't carry the unbearable weight of incredulity, not when the encounter of sense with noumena creates such utile and beautiful phenomena however much our minds might try to subvert this cold clear line of logic because its conflicts with the intellectual tenor of today's literati, who—after much calculation and deliberation, followed by detailed laboratory and field experiments—have concluded that there is no God and that we are products of pure chance alone (which means it must be by pure chance alone that they've arrived at their conclusions).

Our carnal carvings also revolt against the hints of a Creator, because He comes heavy-laden with moral implications. What an irony! These are the same carnal cravings that, consuming us with pleasure, point to the Creator's love for us. After all, from whence did these cravings and urges arise? Why is nature so abundantly equipped to fulfill them? And why do they feel so good being fulfilled?

In simpler, more vulnerable moments, when we're humbled enough by our own self-infidelity to crawl under the barriers of pride and passion and heed the bone-aching cries of our heart, only then will the raw, naked beauty that's in nature *when it doesn't have to be* sing with unmistakable lyrics and soothing hopeful notes of something that only hearts, not minds, can hear. (Do ants appreciate the sunset, or rats the brief artistry of a butterfly?)

Humans can live on three or four types of fruit, three or four types of vegetables, three or four types of grains. So why do hundreds of varieties sprout out the ground and dangle their tangy spasms before our noses? Natural selection didn't demand it. Why do vitamins and minerals and other nutrients come prepackaged in outlandish and outrageously wonderful flavors, textures, shapes, colors, and tastes? For the birds and the bugs? Does a bacterium lick its lips from the taste of the peach it rots?

Don't be a fool. If someone cracked the glass and slashed the *Mona Lisa* at the Louvre, do those gashes diminish the love Leonardo da Vinci first put into the painting? It's tragic that at times crops are so dry that the birds eat only scarecrows, but there can be no famine without first the fields of wheat and corn. And what does the wheat and the corn (and the rye and barley and soybeans and rice) say about the One who first wrapped their seeds in the shell before water, dirt, air, and sunshine lifted the stalk out of the earth and covered it with a sweet crop that, toasted, tastes so good in our mouths and fits so snugly and healthfully in our cells?

Sure, lush fields of grain don't validate the moral argument for God's existence, any more than the thick, sweet air over orchids vitiates a priori materialism. It's readily admitted that the intense pleasures of sex don't prove that God created us as free beings, nor do sunsets reveal the limits of logic and reason to know God's love. And even the child unmodified doesn't show that Christ died on the cross. Don't read more into what's out there than what is.

Don't read less, either.

"But ask now the beasts, and they shall teach thee; and the fowls of the air, and they shall tell thee: or speak to the earth, and it shall teach thee; and the fishes of the sea shall declare unto thee. Who knoweth not in all these that the hand of the Lord hath wrought this? In whose hand is the soul of every living thing, and the breath of all mankind" (Job 12:7-10).

---

[1] Arthur Schopenhauer, *The World as Will and Idea*, trans. Jill Berman (London: J. M.

Dent; 1995), p. 4.

[2] *Ibid.*

[3] Plato, *The Republic,* trans. Desmond Lee (New York: Penguin Books, 1987), p. 317.

[4] George Berkeley, *On the Principles of Human Knowledge,* excerpted in *The Speculative Philosophers,* ed. Saxe Commins and Robert N. Linscott (New York: Random House, 1947), p. 254.

[5] Schopenhauer, p. 12.

[6] Augustine, *The City of God,* p. 217.

[7] *Ibid.,* p. 254.

[Chapter 7]

Fundamental Constants

Man," wrote Russian Joseph Brodsky, "is more frightening than his skeleton."[1] (Woman more than hers, too, and maybe even more so.) Carpalia alone can't twist garrotes, gumless teeth don't bite (or slander), and what can *Ossa cranii* covet of another's? Bones remain quiet, serene, and stable; skeletons symmetrical, balanced, and benign. It's only when flesh and blood are attached . . .

If every effect has a cause (how axiomatic!), what's a priori the Holocaust, the Peloponnesian War, and the Rape of Nanking? What enduring double helix dangles murder, pillage, and conquest from the family tree? Evil is so tolerant, so unbiased, without a racist taint! (The toilets of hell have never been segregated.) Time hasn't refined humanity, only our weapons. Increased knowledge hasn't polished our morality, only our excuses for immorality. It's no mean feat, being able to wipe out life on the planet 50 times over. (A hundred times over would be even more impressive, but as Goethe wrote: "Dear me! How long is art!/And short is our life!"[2]) Evil evolves; only goodness has kept its gills.

It's the first law of moral thermodynamics: *Evil is squared in direct proportion to the bad intended, and cubed in direct proportion to the good.* Marx wanted proletarians to lose their chains, not wrap them around one another's necks. The Gospels command us to love our enemies, not burn them at the stake. Henry VIII wanted only a son, not Sir Thomas More's head.

"By this," said Jesus, "shall all men know that ye are my disciples, if ye have love one to another" (John 13:35). *Fox's Book of Martyrs* recounts some professed disciples of Christ sharing that love with one another. "He was beat with their fists. He was beat with ropes. They scourged him with wires. He was beat with cudgels. They tied him up by the heels with his head downwards, until the blood started out of his nose, mouth, etc. They hung him by the right arm until it was dislocated, and then had it set again. The same was repeated with his left arm. Burning papers dipped in oil were placed between his fingers and toes. His flesh was torn with red-hot pincers. He was put to the rack. They pulled off the nails of his right hand. The same repeated with his left hand. A slit was made in his right ear. The same repeated on his left ear. His nose was slit. . . . They made several incisions in his flesh. They pulled off the toe nails of his right foot. The same they repeated with his left foot. He was tied up by the loins, and suspended for a considerable time. . . . During the whole of these horrid cruelties, particular care was taken that his wounds should not mortify, and not to injure him mortally until the last day, when the forcing out of his eyes proved his death."[3] All this, even after Jesus told His followers to love one another. (Imagine the consequences if Jesus had said, "By this shall all men know that ye are my disciples, if ye just *like* one another"?)

Besides heavenly commands to love, there are earthly commands to hate. The Nuremberg and Eichmann trials revealed, for instance, that if a Jew showed any resistance, "the Nazis tortured not him, but his or some other Jew's children. An infant would be torn into two by its legs in front of its parents; a child's head would be smashed against a tree and the bloody remains handed to the mother; a teenage girl would be raped and then impaled on a bayonet while her brothers and sisters were forced to watch."[4]

Heavenly commands to love. Earthly commands to hate. What's the difference after being filtered through the human mind?

Such darkness, though, remains blatant and easy. Even against a black hole it taunts us with a pigskin tongue. But these grisly snippets are not exceptions to the rule; they are the rule. And if sung the right lullabies, and/or suckled on sour enough milk, and/or prompted by "love" for God, and/or incited by duty to country, and/or nudged by hunger, who wouldn't do the same, even worse? How quickly the conscience flees at the stomach's low growl; how effectively gastric juices erode even the most galvanized axiology. And what remains afterward but base and bottom stripped of conscience and coating that expose nothing but a cauldron of neurotransmitters, synapses, and blood that brew a brooding *Geist*-like vapor!

Nevertheless, such outrageous evils, however offensive (even to the incestuous), are only symptoms—individuated or collective spasms—that reflect the odd archetypical twist within us that would prompt us to gouge out another's eyes once the straitjacket, bleached into local colors of shame, is shed.

After all, when the power lines die and the lights go down in the city, the streets fill with what? Looters or philanthropists?

When Gyges donned the magic ring that enabled him to become invisible at will, did he not seduce the queen, kill the king, and seize power? (What would you expect him to do? Steal from the rich and give to the poor? Replace tyrants with philosophers? Rescue damsels in distress?) Was Gyges especially evil, or did he not just slip into the moral default mode, in which we'd all be but for the artificial constraints in which we are housed?

According to Newton's first law of motion, an object in motion will continue in motion and in a straight line unless acted on by an outside force. The law doesn't explain what direction that straight line is heading in, or why. The first law of moral motion does—and it says that, unless acted upon by an outside force, moral motion is always downward, if not in an absolute straight line, then in one straight enough nevertheless.

Political theory offers a parallel. In the seventeenth century Thomas Hobbes argued that in a state of nature (human existence in a mythical state prior to civil government, society, and law) humanity lived "in a war of all against all" in which humanity had the right to anything it need do in order to best survive. Good and evil were defined only through a harsh survivalist ethic: Whatever aided personal durability was "good," and whatever threatened it was "bad." Fraud and force were the canonized virtues in the state of nature, where life was "solitary, poor, nasty, brutish, and short."

Only a powerful, absolutist sovereign with total authority, Hobbes argued, could bring order and civility to such selfish, egotistical, and violent beings. That sovereign (a single individual or a body) is "that great LEVIATHAN,"[5] and he retained unlimited hegemony over every subject in his dominion, who conceded all their rights in order to receive the stability and security that LEVIATHAN offers.

However extreme, the Hobbesian position is revelatory, embarrassingly so. It says that human moral nature requires something usually corrupt, inefficient, oppressive, and self-serving itself (that is, government) merely to keep people from an incessant "war of all against all," the moral default mode. LEVIATHAN doesn't *change* people. Using the threat of force ("terror," Hobbes calls it), LEVIATHAN simply makes them *act* more restrained, less blatant and open in their expressions of fear, egotism, and violence. How ironic (and more revelatory) that even with LEVIATHAN's sword (or sometimes because of it) life for millions remains "solitary, poor, nasty, brutish, and short" anyway.

Nevertheless, even after climbing out of the warm scar at ground zero or feeling the impress of bootprints on a face (even on someone *else's*) or sniffing the snuffed from distant killing fields, many still cling to the Rousseauian notion that despite greed, violence, selfishness, incest, theft, pedophilia, necrophilia, bestiality, arson, vandalism, fraud, riots, aggression, terrorism, prostitution, corruption, lies, jealousy, guile, pillage, plunder, rape, kidnapping, adultery, torture, war, mayhem, infanticide, parricide, and genocide—humans are basically good. Indeed, if one cracked the human skin, benevolence would drip from the wound because some friendly ghost lurks within the bones of even the worst of us, and we need only to plunge deep within ourselves in order to retrieve this benevolent specter full of smiles, goodwill, and grace.

That position is pestered, though, by rank sensory and/or historical challenges, and the entire twentieth century itself belies it. It's a faith statement, this humanist optimism, requiring some notion of a transcendence inaccessible to empirical verification, which on the crudest level and in almost every direction and dimension busts the friendly-ghost paradigm.

However, a more subtle conundrum rumples another plane, one paralleling the Gödelian paradox that climaxed the chapter "Chemical Dilemma," and this deals with the inability of science to justify itself, because it's unable to step outside itself and view its presuppositions, methodologies, and conclusion from a grander and broader perspective. "How does one judge x," a sentence asked, "when x itself is the very criterion used to do the judging?" Likewise, how can humans judge morality when the precise faculties for judging it (custom, conscience, social norms, civil law) have been sullied by the moral presuppositions that they presume to judge? How can beings, already dumpy with their own moral detritus, fairly weigh questions regarding morality?

Without some exterior source (a mirror, maybe?), we can't see even our own eyes, and even then, after bouncing back off the slick glass, the twin globules first have to parse themselves before becoming accessible to us. (The jury, deliberating, finds itself not guilty.) It's like thinking about thought; the thinking quickly gets tangled within its own thought. (At least one thinks so.)

Thus, whatever the inherent epistemological limits imposed upon us, we return to the crucial question: Does an objective moral standard, a transcendental law of right and wrong, exist? Or is morality a subjective construct only, a peculiar metaphysical dimension mysteriously clinging to pure matter, like pathos added to absolute zero? Either some moral code predates humans—something here to meet us, something that we were poured into (such as curved space)—or morality is derived a posteriori out of human nature, something that wiggles and squirms out of us, like punk rock and Dadaist art.

In the former, humans are judged by that preexistent standard. In the latter, humans ultimately judge that standard because they are the creators of it. They are superior to it, they antedate it, and they have the authority to change or even to abolish it. In short, there is humanity, and there is morality—and humanity stands in relationship to morality as it does either to the sun or to the imagination.

Either way, to agree that torturing children is *evil* or that feeding the hungry is *good* is to imply the existence of a moral dictum defining good and evil, whether that dictum comes prepackaged with the moonlight or dribbles out from sentimentalism and serotonin.

Philosopher A. J. Ayer (for whom ethics is nothing but a branch of psychology and sociology) admits that "we find that argument is possible on moral questions only if some system of values is presupposed"[6] even as he rejects the validity of any moral system because it is, he claims, "outside the scope of argument."[7] (Not a stance someone just beaten, raped, and robbed would find particularly persuasive!)

Actions, to be either moral or immoral, must be contrasted against a system greater than themselves, one that looms over them in presumptive judgment. The concepts of "good" and "evil" demand, by their existence alone, a *standard* of good and evil, a mere definition if nothing else. Otherwise, either to beat a woman to death or to pull her from a burning wreck is, morally at least, no different than selecting chunky peanut butter over creamy.

Australian Brian Medlin has proposed an ethical egoist philosophy which says that everyone ought to look out for one's own interests and disregard those of others except insofar as their interests contribute toward one's own. He claims that to come to any conclusion in ethics, you must have at least one ethical premise, something to start with. In other words, a standard. Morals demand standards as a corpse does death. The mere categories of good and evil imply, either explicitly or tacitly, a moral norm that transcends individual taste. Otherwise, if individual taste leans toward molesting children, then the act must be deemed morally acceptable. But it's not, and everyone knows it's not, because the act itself is judged and condemned by a standard prior to and above it.

Whatever fabric composes its contours, whatever hues and tones sculpt its visage, whatever weights, angles, and lines define its center, that standard (or any other one) is like the weather—it's always there.

Moral neutrality for moral beings is as impossible as spatial neutrality is for spatial ones. Having mass and taking up space, spatial entities such as ourselves—no matter where we go, even to the darkest corners of the cosmos—will always be in some *spatial* relationship to the earth, to the moon, to Betelgeuse, to every other spatial object, regardless of how distant or remote. To claim moral neutrality is to make a moral claim. To watch one man murder another and, though capable of stopping him, you—claiming neutrality—don't intervene is to act with overt moral consequences. Not taking a moral stance on, for instance, racism—refusing to condemn or to approve it—is taking a moral stance on racism. By not passing judgment, you pass judgment. By choosing not to choose, you make a choice. The very act itself contradicts what it claims.

But why should human beings, supposedly mere "matter and the void," have any moral standard, even one that judges child molestation harshly? Though (admittedly) the bar is pretty low here (even the word "low" automatically demands some prior standard—low compared to what?), where did the bar itself first come from? And why do only humans—as opposed to eagles, elephants, and sheep (more "matter and the void")—feel obligated to navigate around it?

The questions get even more difficult when the bar is shoved, heaved, and ratcheted all the way up to integrity, honor, valor, prudence, self-sacrifice, kindness, faithfulness, and honesty. There the metaphysics of morals becomes more grainy and diaphanous than in the obtuse grunge of child abuse. It's not hard, in one sense, to understand why most cultures prohibit rape, murder, theft, or sex with children. The standard behind those proscriptions could be derived from the same stark, cold materialism that sets emission levels for diesel engines.

But how have these other concepts (integrity, kindness, honor, valor, prudence, faithfulness, honesty, which are not necessarily related to survival or might even mitigate against it) been wedged into the human paradigm? From whence came they? Animals in the jungle wouldn't last long if honor, self-sacrifice, and love usurped their instincts. (What monkey would hand a banana to a wounded lion?)

In the Darwinian model the matter that mutated toward mercy, forgiveness, and self-sacrifice should have been buried under 20 feet of muck—somewhere between trilobites and *Australopithecus*. Its phylogenic bough should be a dried-up twig ending with a cold dead bud, not a robust branch exploding into a spout of rich foliage at the tree's apogee. Food (not forgiveness), water (not mercy), and shelter (not self-sacrifice) satisfy basic survivalist needs. Ethics is an inexplicable development among those deemed the fittest to survive, those who have reached the topsoil and beyond.

Obviously some moral code, some unwritten law, transcends the pleasure principle—that ethical metaphysic of empiricist philosophy in which "good" is what gives pleasure and "bad" is what gives pain. However orgasmic, humans do get sideswiped by some moral awareness that trumps their sensory organs and flushes away the rush of endorphins—something that people, though arthritic with culture, society, and personal experience, universally grasp if only erratically follow.

"Think of a country," wrote C. S. Lewis, "where people were admired for running away in battle, or where a man felt proud of double-crossing all the people who had been kindest to him. You might just as well try to imagine a country where two plus two made five."[8]

And even if the one who fled in battle or double-crossed those who were kind derived pleasure from these acts, the acts themselves stand condemned anyway, regardless of the pleasure derived from them and maybe even more so *precisely because of that pleasure*. But condemned by what? What jury, what judge, what standard? Obviously by one that transcends hedonism and that defines good and evil by something more than the mere quanta of chemicals pooled up at nerve endings. A standard perhaps so high, deep, precise, and unyielding that even the best are belittled before it? Maybe the bar is strapped across a splice of space where, standing on their tiptoes and extending their muscles until the ligaments snap, the saintliest stretch in futility? It's not so far-fetched a notion (that of this extreme standard), not really, not when nature itself as revealed (ironically enough) by science rattles the dice before us.

Centuries before Christ the Pythagoreans waxed effusive about "the music of the spheres," a savage image actually, for from within the borders of the atom to coldest folds of curved space, the harmonies, the balances, and the orchestrations have proved musical notes too bumbling, too flat, and too outrageously gangly (like wrapping postulates in cellophane) to be an apt metaphor of cosmic relationships.

Take, for example, the nuclear force, which holds atomic nuclei together. The margin of error is so small that the slightest shift in strength—a burp, even—and human life (at least as we know it) would have never come from the dust. "In a world where the nuclear force were a few percent stronger," wrote physicist-mathematician Paul Davies, "there would be virtually no hydrogen left over from the big bang. No stable stars like the sun could exist, nor could liquid water."[9] Neither, of course, could we.

A few percentage points deviation, however, is crude and almost haphazard compared to the frightfully small margin allowed for forces within stars themselves, which are so delicately balanced that a deviation of $1/10^{60}$, a fantastically small number, would have not allowed our sun to form (which means we wouldn't have either). This incredible balance is another one of what Davies calls the "seemingly miraculous concurrence of numerical values that nature has assigned to her fundamental constants."[10]

There's more, such as the "seemingly miraculous" fundamental constant between gravity (which pulls objects together) and the force of the big bang (which pulls them apart). "Had," wrote Davies, "the big bang been weaker, the cosmos would have soon fallen back on itself in a big crunch. On the other hand, had it been stronger, the cosmic material would have dispersed so rapidly that the galaxies would not have formed. Either way, the observed structure of the universe seems to depend very sensitively on the precise matching of explosive vigor to gravitating power."[11]

How precisely matched? If this balance had been off by $1/10^{60}$, we couldn't exist. "To give some meaning to these numbers," he wrote, "suppose you want to fire a bullet at a one-inch target on the other side of the observable universe, 20 billion light-years away. Your aim would have to be accurate to that same part in 10^{60}."[12]

Now suppose that the moral components of the universe were just as precise, just as fundamental, as the physical one presented here. After all, the universe itself, by default, does come with moral components—it has to. As long as morally aware beings such as we exist within its matrix, moral neutrality is no more possible for the universe than for us. Even if it is cold, impersonal, godless, the universe would still have definite moral implications and consequences for beings whose fate is ultimately determined by the nature of the universe, whatever that happens to include.

Centuries ago Roman orator Cicero, putting words in the mouth of a Stoic philosopher, wrote: "He goes further, pressing the argument more closely: 'Nothing which lacks a vital spirit and reason can bring forth from itself a being endowed with both life and reason. Therefore the universe is endowed with life and reason.' He also pressed home his argument with his favorite technique of the simile, like this: 'If flutes playing tunefully were sprouting on an olive tree, you would surely have no doubt that the olive tree have some knowledge of flute-playing; again if plane trees bore flutes playing in tune, you would likewise, I suppose, judge that plane trees were masters of the art of music. Why then is the universe not accounted animate and wise, when it brings forth from it creatures which are animate and wise?' "[13]

And why is it not accounted moral, too, since it has brought forth moral beings? After all, moral beings could no more emerge from an amoral universe than the *Sonata No. 4 in E-flat Major* could have emerged from a statue of Beethoven.

And what if that moral universe, then, also happens to include fundamental *moral* constants just as finely tuned as its physical ones? What if its moral margin of error were just as unyielding, just as intolerant of deviation, as the forces that precariously balance the stars? Before such a standard—so delicate, so refined, so precise and intractable—we can only blunder and blubber like crude, immoral brutes who are just as incapable of appreciating that standard (much less following it) as apes are of appreciating trigonometry (much less computing the cosine).

Such a "seemingly miraculous concurrence of numerical values that nature has assigned to her fundamental constants" doesn't, of course, *prove* that moral parallels just as fundamental or constant exist, any more than the nature of our skin *proves* that large sharp objects should never be thrust against it. However, if moral laws do come prepackaged with physical laws and if these fundamental *moral* constants are as precise as the physical ones, what would they be? What would they require? And who could stand before them?

Something that reflects $1/10^{60}$ in precision doesn't, after all, leave much wiggle room for beings whose moral choices arrive in much rounder ratios.

Also, how fair would it be to be judged by such a standard without knowing what it was? Why would God (Who else?), having raised the bar so high, then do something clearly below that bar, such as condemn beings for violating a law that they never knew? Would He not by so doing condemn Himself? The only way out of this paradox would be, it would seem, for Him to reveal that morality.

And what if He has revealed to us moral constants, not in numbers, not in formulas or equations, but in an epochal expression of self-sacrificing, self-denying love? What if the moral equivalents of these unyielding physical balances were personified in Jesus Christ, whose every word and act funneled all the fundamental moral constants of the universe into one life? What if the Creator—God incarnated in Jesus Christ—became meek, humble, and lowly, forever exposing pride, self-exaltation, and selfishness as violations of universal morality? What if, having emptied Himself into humanity, God in the flesh lived only to benefit others, even others who hated Him for His meekness, His humility, His lowliness, yet He loved them anyway because such unconditional love—more than gravity or the strong nuclear force or electromagnetism—steadies the edges of the cosmos?

Suppose that, though always tempted, He *never once* succumbed to greed, to lust, to jealousy, and to self-serving because He Himself had set the bar above them? Suppose that He never deviated from the path of perfect righteousness, perfect holiness, perfect obedience, because perfect righteousness, perfect holiness, and perfect obedience is what His own law demanded? What if His life was the divine revelation of the most fundamental moral constant, expressed in humanity as humanity for the benefit of humanity—unselfish love for others even at great personal expense? What if His whole existence was lived solely for the good of those who could do nothing for Him and for the most part would not appreciate what He did for them?

And what if such self-abnegation captures the essence of all truth? "Hereby perceive we the love of God, because he laid down his life for us: and we ought to lay down our lives for the brethren" (1 John 3:16). What if His cry on the cross, "Father, forgive them" (Luke 23:34), remains the supreme expression of moral law: forgiving the unforgivable, and loving the unlovable?

And what if these demands stand as the lowest common ethical denominators of creation, the baseline of all moral existence? And what if any deviation, even $1/10^{60}$, violates this inviolable boundary? Imagine if Jesus—who never sinned, never had an evil thought, never uttered needlessly an unkind word, never put Himself before others—represented the standard by which all our words, thoughts, and deeds will be contrasted against in the stark light of judgment day?

In such an environment our first principles decompose. "Good" and "evil," "right" and "wrong," demand new spellings, new pronunciations, even a new alphabet, because new definitions aren't enough. This standard commandeers all things unto itself, filtering out every other moral center, leaving them a scrap heap of error and illusion.

Sure, our "good" people don't rape or embezzle or murder, but they lust, they covet, they fume (even for $1/10^{60}$ of a second), and in those defining moments evil snivels from within. The good walk lightly on the earth, and though their gentle steps don't muddy our rules, they stomp on God's. A thief's noble choice not to steal the crown jewels doesn't make him an honest man, any more than an honest man's choice not to kill his enemies makes him a saint. "Good" is as relative as the standard that defines it, and a crude, broad standard defines a crude, broad "good." The good are only better than the bad (as Al Capone is to Joseph Goebbels), but that doesn't make them good, not before the divine standard as revealed in Jesus, against whom even the best go belly-up.

What else could they do, when the standard requires that they not retaliate against their enemies but love them, do good to them, pray for them and forgive them? The good don't slap back those who whack first, but do they unconditionally give their left cheek next? Do the best always volunteer the second mile to those who compel them for the first, or offer their cloak to those who sue for their coat? The average obey laws about rape, incest, murder, theft, but who fares perfect against covetousness, jealously, selfishness, and lust, especially when those birds sing sweetly in every skylight window? Who always lives for the good of those who hate and hurt them? Who remain innocent when a spasm of selfishness or hatred or jealously or anger is marked as transgression? Tough standards for a race whose default mode involves looting.

Contrasted against such stark white (the moral background of the cosmos), our stains appear in the fullness of their filth despite the dirt in every eye. If righteousness demands that everything Jesus said to do be done, and if evil is first manifested, not behind the bebop alley or smoke-stained shade but merely by stumbling in the penumbra of Christ's words, then the shadows of even the best are blighted with moral darkness. If anger or jealousy or covetousness breaks divine law, then what's the legal status of a planet where these emotions don't remain as silent chemical processes hidden behind bone but often climax in acts that violate even our hack standards?

How would a God who, while in the flesh revealed only love, mercy, and kindness, view a world in which hatred, vengeance, and oppression are incarnated with the morning dew? How would a God who emptied Himself for the good of others regard a world whose axis is oiled by exploitation and greed? How would a God who healed those who suffer view a world in which violence is as common as rodents? How would He who forgave the unforgivable appraise a planet on which whole peoples are mobilized by vengeance? Or having revealed absolute moral purity, how would He look upon an existence where lust lacquers all cultures? How would a God who, through Jesus, revealed His perfect moral standard, view a world in which every person has flouted that standard, many to extremes of horrifying barbarity and shamelessness?

He views it with unconditional love, that's how. To do otherwise would violate His own fundamental moral constants. Christ died, not despite our violence, impurity, evil, and vengeance, but *because* of them. It was *despite* them that He *loved* the world, but only *because* of them that He *died* for it. We had fallen so far below the standard that only the death of one equal to God could atone for what we had done and, by so doing, had become.

Again, if evil is defined not by whatever is morally vogue (after all, for much of history slavery wasn't considered an evil) but by God's eternal and unchanging law, then everyone from Nero to Hitler, from Mother Teresa to Gandhi, have failed, often miserably—some more miserably than others, however.

But where the world committed rape (not just lust), murder (not just hate), thievery (not just covetousness), Jesus did none of these (even those in the parentheses), and the great mystery is that God allows His perfect record to stand in the place of those who have committed all of these. Before our own laws we fall short; before God's we're not even on the charts, which is why Jesus offers His moral accomplishment in our stead so that all who accept this gift can be accounted as if they had reached it themselves. In Jesus the fundamental moral constants that the world has fiercely defied have been met and satisfied. The essence of the gospel is that from the worst of us to the best of us God offers Christ's satisfaction of the divine standard as a heavenly gift to very earthy creatures in order that they can stand before God in the perfection of Christ Himself, regardless of what their own imperfections have been.

"Now we know that what things soever the law saith, it saith to them who are under the law: that every mouth may be stopped, and all the world may become guilty before God. Therefore by the deeds of the law there shall no flesh be justified in his sight: for by the law is the knowledge of sin. But now the righteousness of God without the law is manifested, being witnessed by the law and the prophets; even the righteousness of God which is by faith of Jesus Christ unto all and upon all them that believe: for there is no difference: for all have sinned, and come short of the glory of God; being justified freely by his grace through the redemption that is in Christ Jesus: whom God hath set forth to be a propitiation through faith in his blood, to declare his righteousness for the remission of sins that are past, through the forbearance of God" (Romans 3:19-25).

Motivated by unconditional love, God has not only revealed His standard but also provided us the means to meet it, the righteousness of Jesus Christ, the righteousness that came from His perfect compliance to the standard that, otherwise, would condemn everyone else.

Instead, for everyone else Jesus faced that condemnation, bearing upon Himself the consequences of our evil while offering us the consequences of His goodness, which is the promise of an existence with none of the things that grind away at this one now.

And He presents this promise as a gift (imagine the audacity to think that one could earn it!) to all who will take, embrace, and make it their own. Otherwise, what life offers us is ultimately death. In contrast, what

His death offers us is ultimately life—eternal life for beings who are, indeed, more frightening than their skeletons.

---

[1] Joseph Brodsky, *Collected Poems in English* (New York: Farrar, Straus and Giroux, 2000), p. 104.

[2] Johann Wolfgang von Goethe, *Faust* (New York: W. W. Norton Company, 2001), p.17.

[3] *Fox's Book of Martyrs,* ed. William Byron Forbush (New York: Holt, Rinehart, and Winston, 1965), pp. 152, 153 .

[4] Max Dimont, *Jews, God, and History* (New York: Signet Books, 1962), p. 383.

[5] Thomas Hobbes, *Of Common Wealth,* in *The World's Great Thinkers: Man and the State: The Political Philosophers* (New York: Random House, 1947), p. 7.

[6] Alfred Jules Ayer, "Critique of Ethics and Theology," in *Language, Truth, and Logic* (New York: Dover Publications, 1936), excerpted in *Philosophy: An Introduction Through Literature,* ed. Lowell Kleinman and Stephen Lewis (New York: Paragon House, 1992), p. 310.

[7] *Ibid.*

[8] C. S. Lewis, *Mere Christianity* (New York: Simon and Schuster, 1996), p. 19.

[9] Paul Davies, *God and the New Physics* (New York: Simon and Schuster, 1983), pp. 187, 188.

[10] *Ibid.,* p. 189.

[11] *Ibid.,* p. 179.

[12] *Ibid.*

[13] Cicero, *On the Nature of the Gods* (London: Oxford University Press, 1997), in *The Book of the Cosmos,* ed. Dennis Danielson (Cambridge, Mass.: Perseus Publishing, 2000), p. 53.

Chapter 8

The Eternal Divisor

Writing about a butterfly that quivered inside his clasp like a flame denuded of heat, Joseph Brodsky mourned over the insect's brief existence:

> . . . the date of
> your birth and when you faded
> in my cupped hand
> are one, not two dates.
> Thus calculated,
> your term is, simply stated,
> less than a day."[1]

Yet, if the truth be known, Brodsky's lament was over, not the insect, but himself and the nihilistic ratios that proportioned his life, the Malthusian computations that—no matter how artfully fudged or fervently prayed about—always added up to zero. "It's clear," he said to the flashy lepidopteron (overdone, even by street-walker standards), "that days for us are nothing, zeros."[2] And zero added to zero 365 times, then multiplied by 60, 70, 90, or even 930 ("And all the *days* that Adam lived were nine hundred and thirty *years*" [Genesis 5:5]) always equals zero.

What Brodsky sensed, as the butterfly created "a frail and shifting buffer"[3] between him and nothingness, was the indifference between his years and the butterfly's day when divided by eternity. Over this divisor—his years, the insect's day, Adam's days of years—what's the difference? All are swallowed up by one cold, unknown sum. If, as Galileo said, mathematics is the language of nature, then numbers become genocidal and integers dismal and damning.

"Existence precedes essence," postulated Sartre. But if all human existence is divided by eternity, the lowest common denominator upon which all temporality rests, the continuum upon which all our moments, hours, days, years are plucked off like gray hair—then our lives, any finite existence, must equal zero. The temporal divided by eternity comes to nothing, and what kind of essence can be extracted from nothing? You might as well go to St. Petersburg in order to borrow rubles from Rodion Romanovitch Raskolnikov or to Yoknapatawpha County to buy a mule from Bayard Sartoris.

"There's much that's sad in the joke God played,"[4] said Brodsky to the thin pigment between his fingers. Only for us, it's no joke to be numerators over the one denominator that divides our lives into a line of zeros strung out on either side of the decimal point. It is, in the end, to live for nothing. *Hebel* is what the ancient Hebrews called it, "a vapor," "a breath"—act or actions that come to naught. The word can apply to the emptiness of an idol, to a god of stone or wood (only a few atomic orbits from dust and ash). Individual acts of *hebel* are frustrating and useless enough. But what if *all* our acts—added, counted, and tallied—terminate in zero? What's to the left of the equal sign if what's to the right means nothing?

Of course, "nothing" is something. *Nothing* is a word; it has definitions (lots, in fact). In *Webster's Encyclopedic Unabridged Dictionary of the English Language* (1989), "nothing" has 13 meanings. *Thirteen!* Anything with 13 meanings must mean something, even if not (in this case) anything we want for our lives, not with all the pain, fears, trials, and traumas that precede it, all the parts of the whole that when pasted together come to a big fat 0. Something's terribly wrong with this math, but if numbers don't lie, then humans have to, at least to themselves.

"Man is nothing else than his plan," wrote Sartre. "He exists only to the extent that he fulfills himself; he is therefore nothing else than the ensemble of his acts, nothing else than his life."[5] For Sartre, human life has no meaning a priori. Only that which we bring to life defines life. All that we are, or ever could be, is a posteriori only. However finely woven are the threads that clothe our worldviews or however precious the ornaments that primp and prink our days or however eloquent the verses that mine our movements—the numbers still crush them all. Whether an age of heroes or an age of cyborgs, when multiplied by zero (or divided by eternity) the fractions remain hellish, the sums unbearable.

Even if we were able to fashion the meaning of our own lives, able to create the justification for our existence, able to extract viable terms of reference that define who we are and what we mean—so what? No matter how eloquent, refined, or logical our meanings, justifications, and terms are, there was an eternity before us that didn't include them and there's one after just as exclusive, which leaves us in between, heavy-laden with meaninglessness.

Strange juxtaposition, "heavy-laden with meaninglessness"! We think of meaninglessness as a void, absence, a vacuum, but not in this case, because even zero has a meaning—even if it's not one we want for ourselves. Zero, nothing—they're not nouns, adjectives, complements, or predicates that we covet, even though many people proceed upon premises inherent in zero and nothing themselves.

Meaningless itself doesn't quite mean what it means, either. It's a one-word Gödelian paradox, one of those quirky epistemological anomalies that not only exposes the flimsy girders of formal logic but reveals the need for faith—belief in what we can't understand. To modify something with meaninglessness isn't to denude it of meaning, but only to change its meaning. An existence that becomes a meaningless existence is simply a different existence than it was without the modifier draped over it.

Webster defines *meaningless* as "without meaning, significance, or value; purposeless; insignificant." Yet each one of those concepts, "without meaning"; "without purpose"; "insignificant," when applied to anything refashions, not destroys, it. To say that our lives, in contrast to eternity (which swallows them into zero, into nothingness), are meaningless only redefines our lives. It doesn't denude them of meaning, definition, or value; it just gives our lives meanings, definitions, and values that make them hardly worth the angst expended in unfurling them. Camus' famous line about suicide being the only important philosophical question makes flagrant sense. Given the premises upon which much of the modern and postmodern world floats, maybe the only sane are the suicidal.

The bottom line, the harshest fact, is that we are temporal entities in an eternal vat, and we flounder before our fate like beached fish. We're finite, and no matter how intently we twist, tweak, genuflect, and wail, we remain finite—and the finite divided by the infinite leaves nothing behind, nothing to the right (much less to the left) of the decimal point, no remainders to carry over. (Zero is the roundest of numbers.) Poetic images of us as sparks, as dying leaves, as the "quintessence of dust," as vapors, attribute too much to us, at least in contrast to what the nihilistic number of eternity does to us, which with one quick calculation divides us into nothing.

Temporality, mortality, finitude, when contrasted to the ideas of eternity, immortality, infinity, become the cube root of our dilemma. (How flimsy our mettle must be: Though physical, we're nullified by ideas alone.) Maybe that's why Martin Heidegger said that only a God can save us. Maybe that's why Sartre wrote that the essence of man is the "desire to be God,"[6] because without God, or without us becoming God, our fate is hopelessness. As the chorus in *Alcestis* bemoaned in beat: "But Fate is above us all./Nothing avails against Fate."[7]

Without the supernatural, the natural is our eternal and unvanquished enemy. Without something that transcends the confines of science, nature, logic, reason, empiricism, *and math*—without a deus ex machina (one that doesn't need a crane)—the undying grave is to us what "z" is to the alphabet. We're in a losing game for life; some just lose earlier than others. Considering the crumbs left over, maybe it's the dead who have hit the jackpot. The rest of us carry the useless tickets, the empty numbers that sit so stagnant and heavy, in our pockets.

No wonder, then, that Jesus and the Bible writers were so unequivocal about eternal life. Otherwise . . . what?

"Whoso eateth my flesh, and drinketh my blood, hath *eternal life*" (John 6:54).

"And I give unto them *eternal life*" (John 10:28).

"Who shall not receive manifold more in this present time, and in the world to come *life everlasting*" (Luke 18:30).

"For God so loved the world, that he gave his only begotten Son, that whosoever believeth in him should not perish, but have *everlasting life*" (John 3:16).

"These things have I written unto you that believe on the name of the Son of God; that ye may know that ye have *eternal life*" (1 John 5:13).

"Howbeit for this cause I obtained mercy, that in me first Jesus Christ might shew forth all longsuffering, for a pattern to them which should hereafter believe on him to *life everlasting*" (1 Timothy 1:16).

"But whosoever drinketh of the water that I shall give him shall never thirst; but the water that I shall give him shall be in him a well of water springing up into *everlasting life*" (John 4:14).

"But now being made free from sin, and become servants to God, ye have your fruit unto holiness, and the end *everlasting life*" (Romans 6:22).

"And this is the will of him that sent me, that every one which seeth the Son, and believeth on him, may have *everlasting life*" (John 6:40).

"Keep yourselves in the love of God, looking for the mercy of our Lord Jesus Christ unto *eternal life*" (Jude 21).

"Verily, verily, I say unto you, He that believeth on me hath *everlasting life*" (John 6:47).

"And this is the promise that he hath promised us, even *eternal life*" (1 John 2:25).

"That being justified by his grace, we should be made heirs according to the *hope of eternal life*" (Titus 3:7).

All these texts end, literally, in "eternal life" or "everlasting life." We can too (and without the quotation marks). But only God can bestow this life, because to go from temporality to eternity demands an endless source of power, *and who else but God can give it?*

Eternal life makes sense in light of the cross; in light of the cross nothing else makes sense but. For what purpose has the Creator of the universe—the one who "made the worlds" (Hebrews 1:2) and in whom "we live, and move, and have our being" (Acts 17:28)—become incarnate in human flesh and in that flesh died? That we ultimately rot, like road kills? If so, then Christ should have heeded the rabble's cry: "He saved others; himself he cannot save. If he be the King of Israel, let him now come down from the cross, and we will believe him" (Matthew 27:42). Believe Him about what? If we're marooned in the temporal, then the cross was futile—and we need more futility as we do more greenhouse gases. It's all or nothing at all, because if not given, all we're given is nothing.

The earth is hungry. There's an essential equilibrium, a macabre ecological balance. Whatever we pull out of the earth, the earth pulls back out of us. (Gravity is the ground's incessant feeder.) Peel away the sky; pluck out the sun, the moon, and the stars; vacuum up the cold remnants of space and time—and what remains? Wealth, status, love, success—none are immune to the worms' rapacious burrowings. Dreams (miracles too) don't escape their squirmy jaws. Even if our lives were bountiful, happy, fulfilled—an ascent from one triumph to another, from one joy to another—death leaves it all in a well-trimmed dump.

(And the undertaker becomes a garbage man.) *Teleos* equals *thanatos*.

Most lives, though, are parsed, not into success, happiness, and fulfillment, but into tragedy, suffering, and fear, which ends only when the brain stops getting oxygen. "Therefore, while our eyes wait to see the destined final day," wrote Sophocles, "we must call no one happy who is of mortal race, until he hath crossed life's border, free from pain."[8] What a pathetic existence, when the only sure remedy for pain, fear, and sorrow is cerebral suffocation!

That's why the New Testament comes laced with promises of eternal life, for only the eternal can guarantee restitution. A million years, even a billion years, might not possess enough good moments to make up for the bad. Eternity alone can balance all things out, and then some, because the infinite is more than the finite, and always infinitely so.

In "Sad Strains of a Gay Waltz" Wallace Stevens peered into souls "empty of shadow," into the meaninglessness of lives striving for something so elusive that it evades even articulation:

> There is order in neither sea nor sun.
> The shapes have lost their glistening.
> There are these sudden mobs of men,
>
> These sudden clouds of faces and arms,
> An immense suppression, freed,
> These voices crying without knowing for what,
>
> Except to be happy, without knowing how,
> Imposing forms they cannot describe,
> Requiring order beyond their speech.[9]

A common sadness pervades the species; a universal sigh hisses from its lips, as if squeezed out by gravity (or is something in the water?), even if the sound's muffled by the flat caws of crows or the tickle of brooms. Death alone mutes it. What a paradox: The only thing that ends pain causes so much of it!

If, as Wallace Stevens wrote, voices are crying "without knowing for what," if they can't even describe the void (What color is a vacuum? What

is the viscosity of nothing? How many ridges line the bottom of emptiness?), then how futile all attempts to fill it must be.

Whatever cushions we crudely nail into the bleak corners that cage
and triangulate our lives, "these sudden mobs of men" know (without
words) that happiness is like flatulence and that it vanishes faster than do
dreams, which drip along warm pillows in the dark. And even if nothing
takes happiness away in life, in death it's all sucked out of the air until
there's no breath left to rejoice in—a tough ending for beings who measure time in increments and are unable to touch the eternity that taunts
them with each hard-edged tick.

The most amazing hypothesis ever carried across synaptic clefts is not
that there's a God, but that there's a *loving* God—a God who loves humanity, who loves each person *individually*. The existence of deity itself,
though hardly tautologous, is a conclusion that doesn't require convoluted
inferences, gnarled axioms, and distended predicates to reach. Logic,
without much stretch, leads to a reasonable (if not apodictic) belief in an
Unmoved Mover or an Intelligent Designer or a Demiurge or gods, or a
God. The symbols, the axioms, the inferences work—at least well enough
to make belief in God about as reasonable as belief in other minds.

But no math, no logic, no set of axioms and valid inferences, arrive at
a *loving* God. Science, logic, and reason don't lead to the cross; they can't.
(You might as well use a pocket calculator to parse the *Rape of Lucretia.*)
What axioms, what premises, what logical rules—no matter how tightly
wrenched—culminate at Calvary, at the Creator in human flesh bearing
the pain, the guilt, the punishment of all the evil that has ransacked the
human race ever since evil extracted its first tear?

But if the cross is truth, then it is the most important of all truth. *God
Himself, the Creator of the universe, took humanity on Himself and in that humanity died a death worse than any human has ever experienced, all in order to
give humanity its only chance to live eternally, to escape the clutches of inevitable
death.* Come on! For beings whose compass needle always points toward
the grave (no matter what direction they face), what else matters?

And if the cross is the most important of all truth, then the most
important of all truth has to be told us, explained, described, interpreted,
analyzed, and simplified for us. Otherwise, how could we know it? With
such issues involved—eternal life or eternal destruction for every human—

imagine being left to discover it ourselves? Our scientific and intellectual cognoscenti can't even agree on what life itself is (though it squiggles and squirms under their microscopes). Who, then, expects them to explain *eternal life?*

Not only does the cross have to be told us, it has to be believable, too. (Why bother revealing the unbelievable?) Faith in Christ, though it transcends reason, is nevertheless *reasonable*. (Don't forget the double-split experiment.) It's just not absolute (If it were, why call it faith?), because, given the nature of things, it can't be—not when even certainty itself comes larded with doubt.

Because only a tiny portion, handfuls at most, of the billions who have ever lived or ever will live were at the cross to watch the sun darken (Luke 23:44, 45), feel the earth quake (Matthew 27:51), see the dead rise (verse 52), and observe the water and blood flow from Christ's side (John 19:34)—how could anyone believe in these events other than by faith?

As with any incident inaccessible to our immediate senses (themselves heavy-laden with epistemological suspicion), faith is as mandatory for belief as O is to H_2O. Whether Hannibal's elephantine trek across the Alps or Abe Lincoln's final action in Ford's Theater or Jesus Christ on the cross, we didn't hear the Carthaginians pray, we didn't smell the smoke of Booth's gun, we didn't see the Romans hammer the nails into Christ's hands, so belief in even these events is, of necessity, alloyed with faith—belief in what we can't prove or fully understand, which encompasses almost everything we know or understand. What can we know *for sure* when the very processes by which we know—thought and consciousness—arrive with abysmal unknowns themselves?

That's why faith is required to accept Christ, not just as a Jew crucified by the Romans but as the eternal Son of God, whose death at the cross paid for every earthly evil, thereby allowing those evils to be forgiven by the One whom they have hurt the worst. Even if the words *JESUS CHRIST, THE SON OF GOD, DIED FOR THE SINS OF THE WORLD* were written every day across the sky in every land and in every language by a means that eluded rational, scientific explanation, belief that *JESUS CHRIST, THE SON OF GOD, DIED FOR THE SINS OF THE WORLD* would still require faith.

Those miraculous letters wouldn't make the truth of His death absolute, any more than a voice shouting from the sky in every language and in every land, saying, *"JESUS CHRIST, THE SON OF GOD, DIED FOR THE SINS OF THE WORLD,"* would either. Belief in that truth demands belief about a past event (which we can't see) and a future event filled with promises (which we can't see either—at least for now). All we have is the present, which is continuously shucked into the past, while the future hovers always beyond reach, offering only—when it becomes the present—one certainty, and that is death.

Thus, without the hope of eternal life, a hope that we carry by faith (How else?), what are our lives, what can they mean, what can they be, but sad and pained packets with protein metabolism that propagate other protein packets of the same sadness and pain? Do the children grow up happier than the adults who spawn them and die? Why make more miserable images of ourselves? The most natural thing is also the most selfish. To create—for our own personal satisfaction (Why else?)—people who will surely face tragedy and, inevitably, death (maybe a horrible one) seems self-indulgent at best and criminal at worst.

One doesn't have to be Jeremy Bentham to do the math. *The greatest good for the greatest number?* If so, the calculi make specious the reproduction of the species. Twenty well-fed Western kids to one starving African child? One hundred healthy preschoolers to balance out one with Down's syndrome? What percentages, what ratios, could ever make humanity and its pain cost-effective?

> Here let me die: for to give birth to those
> Who can but suffer many years and die,
> Methinks, is merely propagating death,
> And multiplying murder.[10]

And yet the most amazing thing in creation is that the God of creation knows our pain and sadness not because He sits upon His throne, a feudal lord overlooking His serfdom, but because He Himself experienced our pain and sadness; not because He's the omniscient God, but because He became human and endured more pain and sadness than any human ever could. And it's out of this—His own pain, His own sadness—that the promise of an eternity to atone for ours arises.

If we could look into a mirror so polished and refined that it captured all our fears and reflected within its frame not only what we are now but what the future will make us be, who would not pound the damning glass (though it proves as unbreakable as fate)? No such mirror exists, so instead of being expressed at once, as in the mirror, our lives come sluiced and sliced in painful drips that, when all is said and done, barely leave stains.

"Love not the world, neither the things that are in the world. . . . For all that is in the world, the lust of the flesh, and the lust of the eyes, and the pride of life . . . is of the world. And the world passeth away, and the lust thereof: but he that doeth the will of God abideth for ever" (1 John 2:15-17).

How desperate this flesh and lust must be to love a world so inimical, harsh, and unforgiving to both and to love *the things* of the world, things that coddle our flesh and tickle our lusts before curdling and killing them both. Maybe we love these things because that's all we see, feel, taste, hear, and believe, at least without the promise of something beyond them, something better, even when the hints of what transcends them are in them.

We want permanence, we want stability, we want order. But we cling to a world that offers only the sound of time passing through matter. (Or is that matter passing through time?) Either way, what's left when the noise ends? Lives lived for the sake of life itself? Please! That's like plucking wings off flies. Without permanence, what are our lives other than pathetic expressions of flesh that, even if expressed "rightly" (remember the standard of 10^{60}), can mean nothing in and of themselves? What can sweating, secreting chemicals that sweat and secrete other chemicals that inevitably break down into carbon, mean? If we're numbers, letters, signs in a formula, then reduce a number, shift a letter, remove a sign—and we stop existing.

Leo Tolstoy, through the dying Ivan Ilych, anguished over these questions. "And he ceased crying, but turning his face to the wall continued to ponder the same question. Why, and for what purpose, is there all this horror? But however much he pondered he found no answer. . . . 'Resistance is impossible,' he said to himself. 'If I could only understand what it is all for! But that too is impossible. An explanation would be possible if it could be said that I have not lived as I ought to. But it is impossible to say that,' and he remembered all the legality, correctitude, and propriety of his life. 'That at any rate can certainly not be admitted,' he thought, and his lips smiled ironically as if someone could see that smile and be taken in by it. 'There is no explanation! Agony, death. . . . What for'?"[11]

What for? Maybe no God exists, and thus time lapses into eternity without us, so all that was, is, or will be us gets divided by the one divisor that makes us what we were, are, or will be into nothing. Or perhaps God exists, and through Jesus He has given us reasons to hope for something beyond death as the denouement for all that precedes it. Death answers no questions and solves no existential mysteries. It only soaks the questions in bile and plunges those mysteries to abysmal depths. "Once a man has realized," wrote Tolstoy, "that death is the end of everything, there is nothing worse than life either."[12] But God, through Christ, answers the questions that now shrivel the tongue for the asking.

"I believe," wrote Anselm, "in order that I may understand." Only belief makes faith understandable, and if by faith (How else?) we allow God within the spaces of our own brokenness, if out of our helplessness, fear, uncertainty, we surrender to the Lord, He will provide understanding enough. Faith isn't, as Kierkegaard suggested, a leap *into* the absurd; it's a leap *over* the absurd.

What really is absurd is to live without hope when hope has been so plentifully and desperately offered. By solving the problem of death, Jesus solved the problem of life. By giving something after the grave, Christ gives us something before it—hope. And what greater hope for those trapped in the temporal than the promise of the eternal? Faith is not so much a leap but a step—a firm, humble, intense step—away from certain disaster. Again, why would Christ suffer such a horrendous death in order that we might have life, only to make faith in that death—the sole means of acquiring that life—so hard to have and exercise?

He wouldn't. Which means that the breakdown isn't on God's end, but ours. Lust, passion, pride—these are the witching chords that incite unbelief within us. We want to be left to the flesh even though it hardens into warty squash or softens into unwashed rags. We want to bathe in our senses even though the pool drains dry and becomes as brittle as dead bone. We know these things, we see these things, we experience these things, yet we're so bewitched by flesh that we can't let it go even as we feel it die right on us.

Peel away the intellectual facades, look beyond the stained-glass obstructions, stare into the secret corners of soul, and the reasons for unbelief (not for the inevitable and difficult questions) that you'll see crouched inside aren't social, intellectual, cultural, but carnal. Flesh uses mind to squelch the heart, which cries out for something beyond the incessant stench of mortality. People fear faith, not because they're afraid of living a lie (most know that they're living a lie already), but because their flesh fears it. What's worse? The denial of our flesh, or its demise? The heart says, *Seek the eternal over the temporal, but the heart is often chewed up by the carnal animal within.*

Behind our fleshly groanings rings a soft, incessant voice. If we cultivate it as opposed to squelch it, if we cherish it as opposed to flush it out with hormones (even if we hide that creamy wash behind the hard veneer of science), if we seek to understand what it says rather than block it out with lust dubbed "reason," then this voice will open us to the reality of a God—a Creator who loves what He has created. If we heed that prompting from the little hook divinely embedded right behind the flesh of every human being, then the Lord will lift us from the horizontal into the vertical and into a love that transcends all the reasons to disbelieve and deny, however tenaciously those reasons remain.

We have a choice, the only one that can change the number over the divisor enough so that sum will equal the eternal we all ache for. But only the individual can make that choice. Free will, even more than death, remains one of the most powerful and consequential forces in the cosmos, second only to the love which first allowed that choice and now unceasingly prompts it.

---

[1] Excerpt from Joseph Brodsky, "The Butterfly," *Collected Poems In English.* Copyright © 2000 by the estate of Joseph Brodsky. Reprinted by permission of Farrar, Straus and Giroux, LLC.

[2] *Ibid.*

[3] *Ibid.,* p. 77.

[4] *Ibid.,* p. 72.

[5] Jean-Paul Sartre, *Existentialism and Human Emotions,* p. 32.

[6] *Ibid.,* p. 63.

[7] Euripides, *Alcestis,* in *Seven Famous Greek Plays* (New York: The Modern Library, 1950), p. 278.

[8] Sophocles, *Oedipus the King,* in *Seven Famous Greek Plays,* p. 182.

[9] From Wallace Stevens, *The Collected Poems of Wallace Stevens,* copyright 1954 by Wallace Stevens and renewed 1982 by Holly Stevens. Used by permission of Alfred A. Knopf, a division of Random House, Inc.

[10] Lord Byron, *Cain, A Mystery,* in *Poems of Byron, Keats, and Shelley* (Garden City, N.Y.: Doubleday and Company, 1967), p. 139.

[11] Leo Tolstoy, "The Death of Ivan Ilych," in *The Kreutzer Sonata and Other Short Stories* (New York: Dover Publications, 1993), pp. 57-59.

[12] Tolstoy, in a letter excerpted in Rosemary Edmonds' introduction to *Anna Karenin.*

[Chapter 9]

Either/Or

Hacked by evils that left justice a stump (an amputee of truth), Job bemoaned his sufferings when God, "out of the whirlwind," appeared and asked: "Can you bind the chains of the Pleiades, or loose the cords of Orion? Can you lead forth the Mazzaroth in their season, or can you guide the Bear with its children? Do you know the ordinances of the heavens? Can you establish their rule on the earth? Can you lift up your voice to the clouds, that a flood of waters may cover you? Can you send forth lightnings, that they may go and say to you, 'Here we are'?" (Job 38:31-35).

Of course not. Not knowing what those chains, those cords, were, Job couldn't loose or bind them any more than we, sheaves of computerized papyri later, could loose or bind them either. And though we know more about those chains than Job did, even the mere local "ordinances of the heavens," the clouds, the lightning, the rain—all leave our theories discombobulating in a mixed ignorance that goes much deeper than the weather forecaster's false prophecies about signs and wonders in the sky.

And now atoms, the *Urstoff* of all stuff, the foundation of all that we thought was, might be only a crude view of what is, like squinting at stars and thinking you've breached the edge of the cosmos. Protons, neutrons, and quarks might not have taken us much closer to ultimate reality (that into which all can be resolved and which, in and of itself, can't be resolved into anything else) than earth, air, water, and fire took the ancient Greeks there 25 centuries ago. Instead, contradictions between general relativity and quantum theory (the two pillars of modern physics) have led to the proposal that the elementary ingredients of the universe aren't point particles such as protons and neutrons (as we've been taught for the past century), but one-dimensional strings whose vibrations make up everything from quarks to nebulae.

Matter and energy are, the theory proposes, oscillations of these ultramicroscopic filaments, different "notes" creating different manifestations of matter, just as different vibrations on a guitar string create different music. Matter appears as point particles not because that's what it is, but because our instruments are too crude, too bland and boring, to reveal the strings themselves. (A string is to the size of an atomic nucleus as an atomic nucleus is to the size of the earth.) We would need an atom smasher a million billion times more powerful than what we have now in order to expose strings, if they exist. And they might not.

Nothing's absolute about science or the theories it proposes. What guarantees that formulas won't become myth or that any regnant law won't be usurped by another, which itself gets tossed into the dungeon alongside its predecessors and eventually its successors? Were scientists to find the elusive grand unifying theory that answers all questions, resolves all contradictions, and does so with simplicity, symmetry, and beauty, nothing promises that another theory more symmetrical, simple, and beautiful isn't holed up behind it. Everything needs explanation by something more universal and basic than itself, and then something more universal and fundamental than that, and on and on either in infinite regress or until we reach that which is inexplicable because it was before every explanation and had no origin or antecedent but was predicated on no cause because it was prior to all causes.

Within the postmodern milieu, however, the search for the final theory—the once-and-for-all answer that explains and unifies all physical laws—seems quaint and naive, like a child who, having just been told that babies come from the cabbage patch, peers under the green leaves for a little brother. Postmodernism rejects the existence of any grand unification theory, any overarching metanarrative (religious or scientific).

Postmodernism asserts that only local, contingent, and fluctuating experiences based on personal or social interpretations—nothing else—is what we're made of. There's no staid objective reality, no empirical facts or a priori certainties, but only a complex confluence and conflation of interpretations based on cultural-linguistic signs, words, and symbols that are no more absolute than the symbols themselves.

What, for instance—other than the whim of someone living in a narrow cultural, political, and aesthetic environment a few hundred years ago—makes the red, white, and blue stars and stripes a symbol of the United States? Would not a cougar, a hawk, or a full moon in yellow, blue, and black do?

Because all knowledge is mediated through the symbols of language (words), and because words (symbols) are defined only by other words (other symbols), and these symbols by yet other symbols (other words), we circle in infinite linguistic regress—a kind of a meta-tautology that reveals nothing. If all we can define words with are other words, then we don't really know what words are. Thus, how can they adequately describe reality when the descriptors themselves remain indescribable by anything greater than themselves? If language and its meanings are cultural, social, and political contraptions—nothing more (as they seem to be)—how much stability, objectivity, and truth can we find within them? "The words of things," wrote Wallace Stevens, "entangle and confuse."[1]

For the postmodern, then, not only is the "meta" of metaphysics superfluous, but the "physics" as well. There are no facts, only interpretations, and interpretations are never final, not when dribbled out of something as fluid and leaky as language.

"For twenty-five hundred years," wrote Houston Smith, "philosophers have argued over which metaphysical system is true. For them to agree that none is true is a new departure."[2]

Yet the postmodern premise is as self-contradictory now as when 2,500 years ago Arcesilaus said, "Nothing is certain, not even that." The overarching denial of the absolute implies an overarching absolute: It affirms what it denies because the denial refutes itself. To claim that no philosophy is true is to make a philosophical claim to truth. To assert that nothing is certain (not even that) is to assert a certainty (even about that). Postmodern guru Jean-François Lyotard's cry, "Let us wage a war on totality,"[3] imposes a totality, a metanarrative, upon the world.

To reject a worldview, an absolute, is by default to assert a worldview, an absolute. The claim that something is a lie demands the existence of truth (or at least the belief in the existence of truth). A lie means a *false* statement, but how can something be *false* without truth to contrast against it?

For example, the statement "The sun is made of cardboard" is a lie (an error), but only because the sun is made of something other than cardboard (the truth that makes "The sun is made of cardboard" a lie). Similarly, the statement that "Columbus began to sail across the Atlantic in 1963" is a lie, but only because Columbus began to sail across the Atlantic in 1492 (the truth which makes "Columbus began to sail across the Atlantic in 1963" a lie). Neither could be a lie but for the facts, the truths, that refute them.

The statement "There is a metanarrative that explains the world" is a lie only if, indeed, *no* metanarrative explains the world. In other words, "There is a metanarrative that explains the world" can be a lie—an error— only if a specific truth exists, in this case that truth being that there's no such metanarrative.

Now if the statement "There's no metanarrative that explains the world" were true, as postmodernism claims, then there really is an over-arching metanarrative that explains the world, because the claim that there is no overarching metanarrative that explains the world is, really, an over-arching metanarrative that explains the world. The denial of a metanarra-tive is a broad claim, an expression of the exact totality that postmodernism denies.

To say that everything is contingent, fluctuating, and subjective is to make a noncontingent, stable, and objective statement about everything. It is to express a grand, overarching truth. (You can't get much grander, or more overarching, than to make a statement about everything!) The claim that truth is changing, not absolute, claims an absolute about truth.

Nietzsche's words that "the *erroneousness* of the world in which we live is the surest and firmest fact that we can lay eyes on"[4] states a sure and firm fact about the world we lay eyes on, a statement that he doesn't believe is erroneous. (Thus not everything about the world is, indeed, erroneous.)

To say that reality is subjective, perspectival, illusional, is to make a claim about reality that is supposedly neither subjective, perspectival, or illusional. And to declare even that claim subjective (the one in the previ-ous sentence) is to make yet another objective claim.

Lies don't linger in some mystical metaphysical mist, a semantic pur-gatory unhinged from the world. Lies exist only in relationship to hard facts, to truths, to reality. It's ironic, but without truth—without reality— there can be no lies, just as without health there can be no sickness. Because lies exist, truth must as well.

Though hidden behind postmodernist or deconstructionist locutions like "play of signifiers," "the hermeneutics of suspicion," or "language games," the inevitability of truth—or reality—is inescapable. Each of those phrases is supposed to represent a view of the world, that is, a truth. Those who coined them thought they were representing reality, the way things were. Would, for instance, Ludwig Wittgenstein have coined "language games," which in his mind expressed the inherent subjectivity and limits of language (and hence, knowledge), if he didn't think that the phrase were an accurate representation of reality, if he didn't think it were true?

To deny the reality of truth is as fruitless and as self-refuting as to deny your own existence: The denial refutes itself, because you have to exist to make the denial. The denial of truth makes a claim to truth, because the denial is supposed to be an expression of truth. As long as anything—or even nothing—exists, truth (the explanation for whatever is or whatever isn't) must as well. The existence of truth—as opposed to the knowledge of it (for truth can exist without anyone knowing it)—is a logical necessity.

Martin sits in a restaurant with friends who surround a steaming pizza. Endless speculation and argument about how the pizza got there arise: it evolved by pure chance; Hermes on winged feet flew it in from Olympus; it fell out of a flying saucer; cooks in the kitchen conjured it up; divine fiat created it; the god Marduk spoke it into existence; it's a gift of Guru Maharaji's grace; ad infinitum. Every explanation they propose or accept might be wrong—a sincere mistake, a malevolent deception, whatever. None might ever know how the pizza got there. Or if some believed they did, doubt would always nibble away at the weak corners of their dogma, no matter the evidence for it. Others might give up ever knowing.

Whatever explanation each one accepted, even if each view contradicted the other or even if each person started a religion or a scientific or a political revolution based on his or her own belief about the pizza's origin—even if one or some or all were willing to die or to kill over their belief in the cause, origin, and meaning of the pizza—one thing is sure: Somewhere amid or (perhaps) outside their theories, speculations, and creeds, something caused the pizza to exist, and to know who or what would be to know the truth about the pizza.

The point here isn't teleological (using a pizza instead of a Piaget); it is not *what's* the cause or whether a pizza implies a pizza designer. The point, instead, is only that a cause must exist, and that cause—whatever it was or is (and whether it's knowable or not)—would be the truth about the pizza.

Now, step away from the table—from the tomato, cheese, and champignons—to Martin and his friends and the humanity they represent.

It's hardly a grand leap, either of logic or of faith, to believe that just as an explanation for the pizza exists, so must an explanation for humanity, and that just as the explanation for the pizza would be the truth about the pizza, so the explanation for humanity would be the truth about humanity.

Spinoza once said that in order to live the most perfect life upon the earth, we need to find out the reason we are here and then live accordingly. The concept is soaked in premises, the only certain one being that there's a reason, a cause, for why we're here. Bite your lip, stomp the ground, inhale a thought discarded in the wind. No matter how subjective, contingent, or illusionary everything might appear or really be, we—whatever we are—*are,* but only because something caused us to be.

People might passionately, even to their own (or someone else's) death, argue over the hypotheses of our existence: We're the result of cold dysteleological forces; we're the creation of a loving Creator; we're here because some pagan deity spit us out of his mouth; we're the products of intergalactic seeding (the earth could be a celestial being's cornfield); or we're impressions made by brains in vats and nothing more. The immediate point, again, isn't *what* the cause is but only that a cause must exist—and that cause, whatever it is, makes all contrary claims erroneous.

To reject the ancient Babylonian creation account (that is, the earth is the carcass of the goddess Tiamat, killed in a battle with other gods, a battle that started over Tiamat's sleep being disturbed) means that another explanation—theistic, naturalistic, whatever, even if unknown—must be true. The rejection of any cosmogonic explanation contains the premise of a true one, of truth itself even. (After all, wouldn't that which explains us and the universe be *the* truth?) Thus, truth itself is implicit in every dismissal of a cosmogony.

Various systems (religious, secular, or a mixture of both) make claims about creation that couldn't be right without others being wrong. For instance, the Babylonian version, if true, nullifies the atheistic materialistic model, and vice versa. And maybe all our stories, theories, and sacred texts—no matter how thoroughly tweaked, bowdlerized, and formulated over the vast epochal shifts of human thought—have never brushed even the edges of what happened. Before our origins, logic and math might be crude superstition, and imagination our greatest oppressor. That an explanation exists is axiomatic. (It's inherent in what we dismiss.) What isn't axiomatic is that we will ever know it.

Among the views that have outstretched an arm on the cosmogonic pinwheel (and there are many) is the biblical one, which claims not only to explain our existence but also to answer its greatest problem—the one that, unsolved, makes us and all that we believe and think useless anyway, and that great problem is death, which grinds us all and all whom we love into dirt and even less, while our thoughts dissipate as litter between electrons.

The Bible claims that Jesus Christ has conquered death and that He will undo and even destroy it and that He already has. We wait only for the results to be consummated once and for all. Such claims demand either acceptance as truth—*the* truth—or dismissal as damnable lies. The Bible is a book chock-full of excluded middles.

Either "in the beginning God created the heaven and the earth" (Genesis 1:1), or He didn't. In other words, either the universe was created by the God of the Bible, or it wasn't. (There's no middle ground here, not with this claim.)

Either "the Lord God formed man of the dust of the ground, and breathed into his nostrils the breath of life; and man became a living soul" (Genesis 2:7), or He didn't. Either humans are the purposeful creation of the Lord God depicted in Scripture, or we are not.

John wrote about Jesus: "In the beginning was the Word, and the Word was with God, and the Word was God. The same was in the beginning with God. All things were made by him; and without him was not any thing made that was made" (John 1:1-3). Jesus was the Creator of all things, or He wasn't. To feign some sort of balanced rational compromise or synthesis here is preposterous. Someone either is or is not the Creator of the universe.

Either, as the Bible says, Jesus "was made a little lower than the angels for the suffering of death, crowned with glory and honour; that he by the grace of God should taste death for every man" (Hebrews 2:9), or He wasn't and He didn't. Either Jesus Christ, the Creator, died for the sins of the world, or it's all a lie—and the moral and religious center of Western civilization is based on a myth no more real than Prometheus being bound to a rock for stealing fire from heaven and giving it to humans.

"The last enemy that shall be destroyed is death" (1 Corinthians 15:26). Christ's sacrifice will end death, as the Bible claims, or it won't, which means we either gain immortality from some other source, or we don't at all.

"And if I go and prepare a place for you, I will come again, and receive you unto myself; that where I am, there ye may be also" (John 14:3). Either Jesus will do what He's recorded as saying here, or He won't because those words are lies—either Jesus' or John's (and it hardly matters whose).

The Bible promises, "For, behold, I create new heavens and a new earth: and the former shall not be remembered, nor come into mind" (Isaiah 65:17). Either God will re-create the heaven and the earth, as the text says, or He won't because He doesn't exist or because He can't or because He deceived us by telling us that He will when He won't.

Though often angled, twisted, and bent into nuances beyond the angles, twists, and bends of their letters themselves, these texts nevertheless stake out claims more prime than the earth's curves. And before them all things diminish, because all things divided by eternity (except eternity) become nothing.

"We look not at the things which are seen," wrote Paul, "but at the things which are not seen: for the things which are seen are temporal; but the things which are not seen are eternal" (2 Corinthians 4:18). Between the temporal (whether hours or epochs) and the eternal, a chasm—crepuscular and impassable—has left us in the dust (literally). The promise etched in Scripture is that Christ has bridged that gap for us and that He offers to take us across it with Him. Otherwise, our lives and all that has been painfully packed in and unfurled from them culminate as nothing but a dot on an infinite line, and our temporality remains eternal.

If the promise of eternal life is true (and what could be more important for beings whose existence, otherwise, is measured by the clicker of time clocks?), why would God make it hard to find or even inaccessible? If Christ tasted death "for every man" (Hebrews 2:9), shouldn't He have given everyone opportunity to benefit from that death? According to the Bible, He did: Christ's death covered the world, and that includes not only those who never knew of the cross but also those who have squandered every opportunity to know.

Either way, knowing or unknowing, we're the same: Flesh, and sojourning here with worms and in clay, flesh is such a fragile, fleeting thing. We see its transience in the faces of those we love (and even in the faces of those we don't). Mortality never stops heckling until it chews us up and spits out bones so barren that vultures turn up their ghoulish noses at them.

And yet however fundamental death may be, the cross is more so. It had to be so, because in order for Jesus to give us eternal life He had to get behind death, scoop it up, and uproot it out of the ground rather than hover, mull, and mourn over it as do every human invention, idea, contraption, and philosophy, which—never getting a grip around the grave—can only adorn it with flowers or hew flat platitudes on the fading stones above it.

But Jesus Christ, God Himself in our flesh, not only died in that flesh but also rose from death, showing that God has slipped behind death, has beaten death, has triumphed over death. And when we accept what Christ has done, His victory over death will be ours, too.

Maybe, then, the best reason to accept isn't that of Christ's fulfillment of the Old Testament prophecies such as Daniel 9:24-27, in which six centuries before His birth the date of His sacrifice was predicted with supernatural accuracy, but that without something to unearth the grave and undo death, our lives are off-key odes to meaninglessness, with nothing—not an echo, even—to show for all the preceding racket.

Or maybe the best reason is not that Jesus fulfilled the prophecy of Isaiah 53, which depicted His life and sacrifice more than 700 years before that life and sacrifice, but that deep down a hunger for something gnaws at us no matter how bloated our bellies or stroked our egos. Whatever we do, whatever triumphs we enjoy, and within whatever satisfactions our souls and senses luxuriate, a witching emptiness—an inexplicable angst—blunts every pleasure until every pleasure aches and nothing can heal those dull throbs except death (or God).

The historicity of Jesus, the evidence for His resurrection, or the testimony of the apostles, who lost all things for Christ, are not the best reasons for belief either. A better reason to believe is our need to believe, and a better reason to seek transcendence is our need for transcendence.

Maybe the brooding throbs within us are nothing but instinct aching for what we had and were before death hobbled life. We seek answers now because in the beginning we never had the questions. The things we ask about now—pain, loss, evil—are intruders, after-the-fact perversions of the fact, but the fact is good. To want immortality, to fear our bowdlerization and abridgment by evil (as did Vladimir and Estragon), is an essential expression of our humanity. In contrast, the secular materialistic acquiescence to oblivion (such as Meursault's) is an absurd deviation from that humanity.

The desire, of course, doesn't make the hope true; it just hints that it might be, that these cravings are emanations from the past, reflections of a primal reality deeper than death, echoes of our archetypal selves whispering that we were meant for more than eternal loss.

"Creatures are not born with desires," wrote C. S. Lewis, "unless satisfaction for those desires exists. A baby feels hunger: well, there is such a thing as food. A duckling wants to swim: well, there is such a thing as water. Men feel sexual desire: well, there is such a thing as sex. If I find in myself a desire which no experience in this world can satisfy, the most probable explanation is that I was made for another world."[5] Or something has so terribly twisted this world that sickness, suffering, death—once unnatural to life—have become its fundamentals instead. As thirst indicates that we were made to drink, maybe our desire to transcend mortality and meaninglessness reveals that humanity was originally without either and that to seek the God who can remove both—far from being some flighty phantasmagoric fantasy-world reverie, "a truly transcendental binge"[6] (says Mephistopheles)—is, rather, instinct pointing humanity back to its prime roots. And this is the essence of the cross: to undo our cruel exile in evil, to restore humanity to what was before this aberrant excursion into a realm where flesh was never meant to be. (We were created to live, not to die, forever.)

And if the idea of restoration to an original bliss seems outlandish, it's only because we've been pickled in suffering for so long that what's intolerable—pain, death, fear—have become the givens. Hints of some archetypical utopia (of the child, unmodified) do slip through, but always masked and scarred, if not by the ravages of evil on the external world, then on the tangled wires, off-kilter clefts, and sour chemicals of the internal one (that is, our thoughts). What else could there be, as beings damaged by evil far greater than a mere $1/10^{60}$ deviation from divine law? If anything, the deviations are $10^{60}/1$ *beyond* divine law, which explains the fate of those who fertilize the earth with their flesh and whose dreams become its morning mist.

But no matter how gnarled the genes or ugly the etchings of the mind, the cross promises a new life not just here and now but in a new earth (the old earth restored), where "God shall wipe away all tears from their eyes; and there shall be no more death, neither sorrow, nor crying, neither shall there be any more pain: for the former things are passed away" (Revelation 21:4).

Either He will, or He won't.

He will, He has promised to, and if we can't trust His promises—then whose? And we can know this God and the surety of His promises just as we can know love, mercy, compassion, and goodness. From what do these come, if not from a God who possessed these qualities Himself first before planting them in us? Otherwise, how do protein, carbon, water (amoral material) emerge into love, mercy, compassion, and goodness—realities qualitatively greater than the mere formulas and equations that almost but not quite make us what we are?

Also, what's more complicated, more intricate, more "real"—carbon, protein, water? Or beings made of carbon, protein, and water who can acknowledge God's attributes and, to some extent, reflect those attributes themselves? How ironic that love, mercy, compassion, goodness—too intricate for formulas, too exalted for equations (it takes more than math to make us)—are known better by the heart than the mind, which reveals the limits of the mind to know the higher things!

The mind's good, though, at the lower ones, such as Ivan Karamazov's painful lament about evil. However passionate an excuse, it is still just that—an excuse. (The mind's a specialist at them.) If anything, evil is all the more reason to believe. Otherwise, there are no answers, no purpose, no justice, no hope—nothing but generation after generation of death and suffering until one perfects it enough to destroy itself or until one sputters out and blows away, leaving nothing behind that mourns what came before. But that's only if no God created us, no God loves us, and no God promises to make all things right no matter how impossible that seems to the wires, clefts, and chemicals of our consciousness now. (To different wires, chemicals, and clefts, however, it might appear not just possible but inevitable.)

But until God does make all things right (as He has promised to do), there's Jesus, this same God dying in the flesh in order to make certain and irrevocable the promise. Otherwise, why would God in Christ, in the flesh, suffer more than any human being ever suffered (we suffer only as individuals; He suffered as the whole race) and then not fulfill what His infinite pain promised us?

If having first incarnated Himself into humanity (incredible enough itself) and then in that humanity (but still God) took upon Himself the burden of all our suffering, all our evil, all our guilt, paying for them in Himself as if He had done them all when He had done none—if that isn't enough for Him to fulfill any promise to us, what is? God dying a death worse than any of us but doing it for all of us! How much more do we want? What more do we need?

We know so little, and the little we do know comes diluted with doubt, uncertainty, and fear. But with no uncertainty (yet much fear) we know our need for something more than life now offers—something that's beyond us, that transcends us, though we're not sure what, even if our hearts know, but pride and flesh feed the doubt that pulls us back inside ourselves, into that rash carnality that dies with old animals. How sad to be captured and commandeered by what's so small, so fleeting, so trivial in contrast to the eternal, which is all around us and which beckons us—even if with nothing more than the idea itself, especially when we wake up, half asleep but startled, blood pumping frightfully at the knowledge that one day we'll be gone while the idea remains!

And yet (here's the point of all the pages that precede this parenthesis)—the cross has made eternity more than just an idea, more than just an abstract metaphysical term. The cross has made it a gift for us, more real than everything in the world, because everything in the world wears away. It is as if each turn of the earth on its axis, each revolution around the sun, grinds all things slowly into the ground and leaves only the gift, as eternal as the Giver, the God who cannot lie, who through the sacrifice of Himself has made us a way to escape the fate from which there is (as Sartre wrote) no exit, but from which Jesus says, "I am the door" (John 10:9) and promises all who step through it eternal life.

Either He is, or He isn't; either we do, or we don't.

Either/or . . . nothing else.

---

[1] From Wallace Stevens, *The Collected Poems of Wallace Stevens,* copyright 1954 by Wallace Stevens and renewed 1982 by Holly Stevens. Used by permission of Alfred A. Knopf, a division of Random House, Inc.

[2] Houston Smith, *Beyond the Post-modern Mind* (Wheaton, Ill.: Theosophical Publishing House, 1992), p. 9.

[3] Jean-François Lyotard, *The Postmodern Condition* (Minneapolis: University of Minnesota Press, 1984), p. 82.

[4] Friedrich Nietzsche, *Beyond Good and Evil* (New York: Vintage Books, 1989), p. 45.

[5] C. S. Lewis, *Mere Christianity,* p. 121.

[6] Johann Wolfgang von Goethe, *Faust,* p. 91.